THINGS TO DO IN
LAS VEGAS
BEFORE YOU
DIE

100

THINGS TO DO IN
LAS VEGAS
BEFORE YOU
DIE

• •

LAURA CARROLL AND
ADAM KEALOHA CAUSEY

REEDY PRESS

Library of Congress Control Number: 2015957477

ISBN: 9781681060279

Design by Jill Halpin

Photos by Martin S. Fuentes, except cover photo, by Adam Kealoha Causey

Printed in the United States of America
16 17 18 19 20   5 4 3 2 1

Please note that websites, phone numbers, addresses, and company names are subject to change or cancellation. We did our best to relay the most accurate information available, but due to circumstances beyond our control, please do not hold us liable for misinformation. When exploring new destinations, please do your homework before you go.

DEDICATION

For our parents.

Thank you for inspiring us and teaching us how to have fun.

CONTENTS

Music and Entertainment

• •

Sports and Recreation

• •

• •

Culture and History

● ●

Shopping and Fashion

PREFACE

Las Vegas may have risen to fame as the hotbed of forbidden fun, but in its modern incarnation, there's something for everyone, be they sinner or saint.

Every year, forty million people visit this desert oasis. Whether you're a tourist looking for something new or a local who needs a reminder of why you and two million others call the Las Vegas Valley home, there's something in this book to add to your bucket list.

First things first: Yes, there wouldn't be a Vegas as we know it without a four-mile stretch of concrete and bright lights known as the Strip (which is actually not in the city limits). But plenty more delights paved the way for this worldwide destination that was just a railroad stop when it was founded in 1905. And lots more peacefully coexist with it here in Southern Nevada.

This book serves up a sampling of those natural, historic, and cultural offerings.

You can find world-class dining and entertainment, and that could be on the Strip or in a strip mall. Hike alpine heights just an hour away from the hustle and bustle of the city, or soak up mob and natural history downtown. Try your hand on a casino floor, or show off some moves in a nightclub.

Come any time of year: December, when things are slower, often sees big discounts on spa services, show tickets, hotel rooms,

• •

and dining packages. If it's summer, there are pools galore. Fall and spring are great times for up-close views of the Mojave Desert's beauty. Hotel rooms are generally cheaper on weeknights, and rates can rise exponentially during holidays and big events, especially if it's something worth placing a wager on.

Out West, close is a relative term. It takes more than four hours to drive from Las Vegas to the next major metro area. So some of the entries in this book—particularly natural wonders—are part of the Vegas experience but will require half an hour of driving or more. Plan accordingly.

Those and all our other recommendations came from research, interviews, and lots of personal experience. Las Vegas is dynamic, so if you have any doubts about whether a business is still around, just call ahead. All information was accurate at the time the book was written. We hope *100 Things to Do in Las Vegas Before You Die* whets your appetite by pointing out some must-dos and insider tips. We'll let you create your own experience from there. But, really, do you think you'll get bored?

Join us in sharing your experiences via social media. We're at facebook.com/100thingsLV and @100thingsLV on Twitter and Instagram. Tag your thoughts #100thingsLV.

Good luck—and viva Las Vegas!

• •

ACKNOWLEDGMENTS

In typical Vegas fashion, this whole project started because somebody "knew a guy." Thanks, Henry Brean, for being the guy who knows a guy who wanted to publish this book.

Each conversation with a friend, visitor, or business owner was invaluable to both Laura and Adam. Everyone who has contributed to their Las Vegas experience is truly appreciated.

Adam particularly wants to thank Lynnette Curtis, Sonya Padgett, and Doug Elfman for their honest advice. And Laura wants to thank Jason and her dad, Matt, for their support and encouragement. Both Adam and Laura would like to thank Martin S. Fuentes for his photo contributions.

This is the first book Laura and Adam have written. Neither of them could possibly name every person who has helped them get to where they are. But both want to thank every newspaper editor, school teacher, and occasional online article commenter who— intentionally or not—pushed them to do better.

• •

FOOD AND DRINK

FEAST ON ASIAN CUISINE
IN CHINATOWN

Less than a mile off the Strip, Las Vegas' Chinatown may look different from New York or San Francisco's versions. The Mojave Desert version is more a series of shopping centers along Spring Mountain Road, and more Pan-Asian than China-focused. Head there for great sushi, ramen, Korean barbecue, and other specialties from the Far East, often at a fraction of tourist district costs.

Here are some highlights. No matter where you choose, you're less than a stone's throw away from plenty more offerings.

District One Kitchen & Bar
3400 S Jones Blvd., #8, Las Vegas, 702-413-6868
districtonelv.com

Honey Pig Korean BBQ
4725 Spring Mountain Rd., #K, Las Vegas, 702-876-8308

Sushi Kaya
4355 Spring Mountain Rd., #101B, Las Vegas, 702-257-9496
sushikaya.com

TIP
Try the Beer Share wings or rolls at District One.
Grill your own meat, right at the table, at Honey Pig.
And go for all you can eat at Sushi Kaya.

GET
YOUR COFFEE FIX

Whether you track down a local coffee shop or find the closest Starbucks on the Strip—there are at least thirty-five in a four-mile stretch—you're bound to find your caffeine fix. There are local favorites that have expanded to the tourist corridor, and some that will take you toward the path less trod.

The Beat
520 Fremont St., Las Vegas, 702-385-2328
thebeatlv.com

Makers & Finders
1120 S Main St., #110, Las Vegas, 702-586-8255
makerslv.com

Sambalatte, Monte Carlo
3770 Las Vegas Boulevard S., Las Vegas, 702-730-6700

Boca Park, 50 S Rampart Blvd., #9, Las Vegas, 702-272-2333

6555 S Jones Blvd., #9, Las Vegas, 702-434-2337
sambalatte.com

Sunrise Coffee
3130 E Sunset Rd., Las Vegas, 702-433-3304
sunrisecoffeelv.com

Starbucks
starbucks.com/store-locator/search

The Coffee Bean & Tea Leaf
coffeebeanlv.com/locations

SLINK
INTO A SPEAKEASY

Maybe they're not illegal, or even secret, anymore. And you won't really have to sneak in. But the speakeasy trend of dimly lit but chic backroom social clubs is flourishing in Las Vegas. There's no secret knock or handshake these post-Prohibition days, but you'll be hard pressed to find a doorknob at these places—and reservations are recommended. At one bar inside a bar—the Laundry Room at Commonwealth—you have to get ahold of a phone number to enter. Figuring that out is part of the fun.

Rose.Rabbit.Lie. at The Cosmopolitan
3708 Las Vegas Boulevard S., Las Vegas, 877-893-2003
cosmopolitanlasvegas.com/taste/restaurant-collection/rose-rabbit-lie

The Laundry Room at Commonwealth
525 Fremont St., Las Vegas

Downtown Cocktail Room
111 Las Vegas Boulevard S., Las Vegas, 702-880-3696
downtowncocktailroom.com

Velveteen Rabbit
1218 S Main St., Las Vegas, 702-685-9645
velveteenrabbitlv.com

TIP

At Serendipity, order a Frrrozen Hot
Chocolate, even if it's cold outside.

DEVOUR DELICACIES
OF THE "NINTH ISLAND"

Many Hawaii residents lovingly refer to Las Vegas as the "ninth island," meaning the desert has made them feel right at home. And restaurants and hotels work to keep them coming. You can get poke —chopped raw fish, usually soaked in sesame oil or soy sauce with green onions—and occasionally opihi, a salty-tasting mollusk that clings to rocks in the ocean. Of course there are other dishes popular in Hawaii that have been imported from elsewhere, before the term "fusion" got popular: chicken katsu, kalua pork and macaroni salad.

Poke Express
655 W Craig Rd. #118, North Las Vegas, 702-639-0500

Island Flavor
8090 S Durango Dr. #103, Las Vegas, 702-876-2024
islandflavor808.com

Aloha Specialties at the California Hotel
12 E Ogden Ave., Las Vegas, 702-382-0338
thecal.com/dine/aloha-specialties

TIP
Want more fusion?
Both of these restaurants have multiple
locations, and Fuku has a food truck.
KoMex Fusion: komexexpress.com
Fuku Burger: fukuburger.com

DRINK OR DINE
AT A VEGAS DIVE

It's not all bright lights in Vegas. The city is dotted with watering holes that are dark, dive-y and down-home. Whether it's Atomic Liquors, founded in 1952 and now part of downtown's renaissance, or Four Kegs, whose stromboli got a shout out from Guy Fieri on *Diners, Drive-Ins and Dives*, there's a no-frills bar for you.

Atomic Liquors, 917 Fremont St., Las Vegas, 702-982-3000
atomicvegas.com

Four Kegs, 276 N Jones Blvd., Las Vegas, 702-870-0255
fourkegs.com

Dino's Lounge, 1516 Las Vegas Boulevard S., Las Vegas, 702-382-3894
dinoslv.com

Frankie's Tiki Room, 1712 W Charleston Blvd., Las Vegas, 702-385-3110
frankiestikiroom.com

The Dive Bar, 4110 S Maryland Parkway, Las Vegas, 702-586-3483

The Dispensary Lounge, 2451 E Tropicana Ave., Las Vegas, 702-458-6343
thedispensarylounge.com

TIP
At Dino's, be prepared for some serious karaoke.
Feel free to sign up and belt out your favorite ballad.

GREAT PLACES TO WATCH A GAME

Not dives, but here are some spots that are good
for taking in a game on TV.

The Pub at Monte Carlo
3770 Las Vegas Boulevard S., Las Vegas, 702-730-7420
montecarlo.com/en/restaurants/the-pub.html

Stake Out
4800 S Maryland Parkway #A
702-798-8383

Aces and Ales
3740 S Nellis Blvd., Las Vegas, 702-436-7600

2801 N Tenaya Ave., Las Vegas, 702-638-2337
acesandales.com

GORGE ON
GOURMET CANDY AND SWEETS

So much sugar, so little time. There's plenty to taste here on the boutique sweets scene. Starting with Ethel M—part of the Mars candy empire family tree—you can see liqueur-filled delicacies and much more rolling right off the factory line in Henderson.

For more gourmet chocolate, hard candy, and toffee, check out B Sweet Candy Boutique. And it wouldn't be a truly Vegas business without offering an all-candy buffet for special events.

Last but not least is Popped, offering eclectic popcorn flavors with names like "S'mores," "Dirty Vegas" and "Buffalo Hot & Ranch."

B Sweet Candy Boutique
420 S Rampart Blvd., #240, Las Vegas, 702-798-2979
bsweetlv.com

Popped
9480 S Eastern Ave., Ste. 110, Las Vegas, 702-998-9234
3700 S Hualapai Way, Unit 108, Las Vegas, 702-207-0985
bestgourmetpopcorn.com

Ethel M, Factory and Garden
2 Cactus Garden Dr., Henderson, 800-438-4356

California Hotel
12 E Ogden Ave., Las Vegas, 702-383-3340

McCarran International Airport (multiple locations)
ethelm.com

TIP

For a double dose of fun, check out
Ethel M between November and January
to sample chocolate and take in
the holiday lights in the cactus garden.

STOMP GRAPES
IN SOUTHERN NEVADA WINE COUNTRY

No, it's not quite Napa. But for a taste of wine near Las Vegas, just head west about an hour to Pahrump. This Southern Nevada town is home to a pair of wineries.

Pahrump Valley Winery opened in 1990 and produces zinfandel and syrah grapes in Pahrump, and tempranillo, cabernet sauvignon, and merlot, among others, at its other Nevada vineyards. Free tours and tastings are available in Pahrump ($5 apiece for groups of eight or more). In the fall, the winery hosts a grape-stomping event with tastings, food vendors, and entertainment.

Sanders Family Winery, established in 1988, grows zinfandel and petite syrah grapes at its Pahrump vineyards. The winery offers free tastings seven days a week in its Tuscan-style buildings. Check the events calendar to see if performances—ranging from country bands to impersonators—have been booked when you plan to visit.

If you don't want to drive from Las Vegas, check with the wineries to see if limo or shuttle services are available.

Pahrump Valley Winery, 3810 Winery Rd., Pahrump, 775-751-7800
pahrumpwinery.com

Sanders Family Winery, 3780 E Kellogg Rd., Pahrump, 775-727-1776
sanderswinery.com

KICK YOUR TEA UP A NOTCH
WITH BOBA

This isn't your usual cup o' tea. Boba, also called bubble tea, is an export of Taiwan. It's tea-based, but it's got lots of extras. You can have it mixed with milk, then throw in some tapioca balls, jelly, or fruit. It's sort of like a milkshake with a kick. Kung Fu Tea and Lollicup will remind you of hip ice cream shops. And being Vegas, Café Teaze servers wear lingerie.

Kung Fu Tea
5030 Spring Mountain Rd., Las Vegas, 702-776-7077

Volcano Tea House
4215 Spring Mountain Rd., Las Vegas, 702-207-7414

Lollicup at Town Square Mall
6629 Las Vegas Boulevard S., Las Vegas, 702-260-8988
lollicup.com

Café Teaze
5115 Spring Mountain Rd., Ste. 225, Las Vegas, 702-998-6797

INDULGE
AT A CELEBRITY CHEF'S RESTAURANT

World-class dining is never far away in Las Vegas. In fact, some of the most famous chefs now have opened multiple restaurants on the Strip. Here are ten establishments from those culinary leaders.

Joel Robuchon
Joel Robuchon Restaurant at the
MGM Grand
3799 Las Vegas Boulevard S
702-891-7925
mgmgrand.com/en/restaurants/joel-robuchon-french-restaurant.html

Cuisine: French
Dress code: Formal

Gordon Ramsay
Gordon Ramsay BurGR at
The Miracle Mile Shops at
Planet Hollywood
3667 Las Vegas Boulevard S
702-785-5462
gordonramsayrestaurants.com

Cuisine: American
Dress code: Business casual

Wolfgang Puck
Spago at The Forum Shops
at Caesars
3500 Las Vegas Boulevard S
702-369-6300
wolfgangpuck.com/restaurants/
fine-dining/9044

Cuisine: American
Dress code: Business casual

Giada De Laurentiis
Giada at The Cromwell
3595 Las Vegas Boulevard S.
855-442-3271
giadadelaurentiis.com/vegas

Cuisine: Italian
Dress code: Business casual

José Andrés
Jaleo at The Cosmopolitan
of Las Vegas
3708 Las Vegas Boulevard S
702-698-7000
jaleo.com/las-vegas

Cuisine: Spanish tapas
Dress code: Casual

Todd English
Olives at Bellagio
3600 Las Vegas Boulevard S
702-693-8181
bellagio.com/en/restaurants/
todd-english-olives.html

Cuisine: Mediterranean
Dress code: Casual

Nobu Matsuhisa
Nobu at The Hard Rock
Hotel & Casino
4455 Paradise Rd., 702-693-5090
noburestaurants.com/
las-vegas/experience

Cuisine: Japanese
Dress code: Business casual

Nobu at Caesars Palace
3570 S Las Vegas Blvd.
702-785-6628
noburestaurants.com/
las-vegas-caesars-palace

Cuisine: Japanese
Dress code: Business casual

Emeril Lagasse
Table 10 at the Palazzo
3327 Las Vegas Boulevard S
702-607-6363
emerilsrestaurants.com/table-10

Cuisine: Cajun, Creole
Dress code: Casual, no sleeveless
shirts for men

Michael Mina
Bardot Brasserie at Aria
3730 Las Vegas Boulevard S
877-230-2742
michaelmina.net/restaurants/
las-vegas/bardot-brasserie

Cuisine: French
Dress code: Business casual

Guy Fieri
Guy Fieri's Kitchen and Bar at The
LINQ Hotel and Casino
3535 Las Vegas Boulevard S
702-731-3311
caesars.com/linq/restaurants/
guy-fieri#.VmUji3j09vA

Cuisine: American
Dress code: Casual

GRAB A BITE
AT MOUNT CHARLESTON LODGE

After enjoying a day hiking or sledding at Mount Charleston, make sure to save time to visit the Mount Charleston Lodge. The restaurant serves mountain favorites including a giant Bavarian pretzel with cheese, buffalo burgers, elk burgers, and traditional cheeseburgers. For those with larger appetites, the lodge serves up heartier meals such as ribs, New York steak, and spaghetti and meatballs. Don't forget to order a Mount Charleston coffee as a nightcap to warm you up while you chat with friends by the lodge's central fireplace. It's tradition.

Mount Charleston Lodge, 5375 Kyle Canyon Rd., Las Vegas, 702-872-5408
mtcharlestonlodge.com

TIP
If you're going around the holidays, be sure to make a reservation weeks in advance. There's not much else in the way of dining options at the top of the mountain.

NOSH
AT THE BONNIE SPRINGS RESTAURANT AND BAR

Located south of the Red Rock Canyon visitor's center, Bonnie Springs Bar and Restaurant inside Bonnie Springs Ranch provides good old-fashioned family food year-round. A petting zoo, horseback trail rides, and a duck pond provide outdoor animal interaction for families at the ranch itself. At the onsite restaurant, those who've worked up an appetite playing all day at the ranch or in nearby Red Rock Canyon or Calico Basin enjoy meals in a rustic atmosphere. We recommend the restaurant's cheeseburgers, which are so good that we remember them from way back when we were kids. Try one with an adult beverage at the bar, or sit down with the whole family inside the main restaurant.

Bonnie Springs Bar and Restaurant
16935 Bonnie Springs Rd., Las Vegas, 702-875-4191
bonniesprings.com

WOLF DOWN AN ECLAIR
AT JERRY'S NUGGET

Jerry's Nugget casino in the heart of North Las Vegas has been serving up delicious diner food since 1964. Walk into this diamond in the rough and head straight for the coffee shop to order a homemade eclair. They're huge, filled with creamy goodness, and have a flower on top, to add to the delightfulness. Very old school and very worth the short drive up Las Vegas Boulevard. We promise, you'll thank us later.

Jerry's Nugget
1821 N Las Vegas Blvd., North Las Vegas, 702-399-3000
jerrysnugget.com

LEAVE WORK EARLY
AND HEAD FOR HAPPY HOUR

This one may seem pretty basic, but many people overlook happy hours in a city like Las Vegas. But let us give you focus: In a place that built its reputation on cheap drinks and food deals, the blessed specials abound. These days the food and libations are better than in the past, but at happy hour, the deals are still there. A quick web search will net you lots of ideas on where to go, but the website lasvegashappyhour.net organizes happy hours by neighborhood and gives you the most current details. Whether you're a local on the nine-to-five or in Vegas on business, there's something to help take off the edge.

And don't forget to look for the reverse—or late night—happy hour. Here are few to try.

Herbs & Rye, 3713 W Sahara Ave., Las Vegas, 702-982-8036
herbsandrye.com

The Golden Tiki, 3939 Spring Mountain Rd., Las Vegas, 702-222-3196
thegoldentiki.com

The Peppermill Restaurant and Lounge
2985 S Las Vegas Blvd., Las Vegas, 702-735-7635
peppermilllasvegas.com

TIP
If you eat red meat, the half-price happy hour steak
at Herbs & Rye is a must-have.

SCARF DOWN AN ICE CREAM SANDWICH
NEAR THE FOUNTAIN AT CRAVE

This one's specific for a reason. First, drive to Downtown Summerlin and order a custom ice cream sandwich from CREAM. So, so good. Second, take your custom, delicious sandwich across the drive and park yourself near the fountains outside Crave. The reason for this is simple: it's a great people-watching spot and it's outdoors, so when you inevitably get ice cream all over you from the sandwich, it won't matter as much. Finally, the ice cream shop's name, CREAM, is an ode to a Wu-Tang Clan song, so you get bonus points for completing this one. Cookies really do rule everything around us.

CREAM
1980 Festival Plaza Dr., Las Vegas, 702-272-0072
creamnation.com

IMBIBE WITH A ROCKER
AT THE HARD ROCK HOTEL

It's a Las Vegas tradition to have a drink (or many) at the Hard Rock Hotel's Center Bar. After a show, or before, for many Las Vegans, it's the place to imbibe at the hotel. With its recent facelift has come an expanded bar area, and the hotel has started hosting very famous headliners at the Center Bar on select weekends, complete with free admission. Yes, you heard us, free. So get thee over to the Hard Rock, and look sharp. You never know what rock star will be there enjoying a beverage with you.

Hard Rock Hotel
4455 Paradise Rd., Las Vegas, 702-693-5000
hardrockhotel.com/las-vegas-hotel

TIP
Check concert listings for The Joint and Vinyl. And don't forget to check out memorabilia from rock royalty throughout the casino floor and down the hallway past Vinyl and Pink Taco.

NIBBLE
ON A SHRIMP COCKTAIL

Things have changed at the Golden Gate Hotel in downtown Las Vegas with the resurgence of the area by new casino owners. One thing, though, that has remained constant since the property's inception is its shrimp cocktail. Served in sundae glasses, the shrimp comes with just the right cocktail sauce and lots of free saltine crackers that make this Vegas staple a meal at any hour of the day. Add a little Tabasco sauce to put things over the edge and you can thank us later. We might even see you there.

Golden Gate Hotel
1 Fremont St., Las Vegas, 702-385-1906
goldengatecasino.com

CELEBRATE
OKTOBERFEST—IN LAS VEGAS

You don't have to travel to Germany to celebrate Oktoberfest at the Hofbrauhaus because Las Vegas has one all its own. The Vegas version is an exact replica of the famed beer hall in Munich, complete with rotating, nightly entertainment. Live bands, stein-holding contests, and celebrity keg-tappings make Hofbrauhaus Las Vegas a sure bet for a fun time. Around Oktoberfest the place gets crowded, but the more the merrier at this festive beer hall. Expect to interact with your neighbors during group toasts, and save room for the delicious Bavarian food.

Hofbrauhaus Las Vegas
4510 Paradise Rd., Las Vegas, 702-853-2337
hofbrauhauslasvegas.com

TIP
Wait staff carries some drinks on paddles. Occasionally,
they use those paddles for spankings. So watch your behavior.

EAT AT THE LAS VEGAS CLASSICS

Las Vegas has its fair share of restaurants, from small downtown eateries to the grand, celebrity chef-run places on the Strip. At some point though, you've got to focus on the classics. You know, those places that have been around forever—no small feat in a town that loves to reinvent itself—and for good reason. Think Pamplemousse, Chicago Joe's, anything by Chef André Rochat, Hugo's Cellar, or Piero's. They're run by pros who know how to treat a customer, offer great food, and create an atmosphere.

Pamplemousse, 400 E Sahara Ave., Las Vegas, 702-733-2066
pamplemousserestaurant.com

Chicago Joe's, 820 S Fourth St., Las Vegas, 702-382-5637
chicagojoesrestaurant.com

Andre's at the Monte Carlo
3770 Las Vegas Boulevard S., Las Vegas, 702-798-7151
andrelv.com

Hugo's Cellar at the Four Queens
202 Fremont St., Las Vegas, 702-385-4011
hugoscellar.com

Piero's, 355 Convention Center Dr., Las Vegas, 702-369-2305
pieroscuisine.com

Golden Steer Steakhouse, 308 W Sahara Ave., Las Vegas, 702-384-4470
goldensteersteakhouselasvegas.com

TIP

Luv-It Frozen Custard is a Vegas dessert classic. You can't dine in—just walk up to the window. If it's hot out, expect a line. We recommend "The Desert," which mixes in hot fudge, marshmallows, and pecans.

Luv-It Frozen Custard
505 E Oakey Blvd., Las Vegas, 702-384-6452

GO TO WHITE CASTLE
WEST OF THE MISSISSIPPI

Way before Harold and Kumar cemented White Castle as a pop culture phenomenon, Midwest and East Coast transplants to Las Vegas craved the sliders they grew up with. Local supermarkets sell the frozen kind, but nothing's as good as a White Castle slider fresh off the grill when you really want one. Precious time was carved out for stopping by White Castle during trips back home, and finally, after decades of yearning, Las Vegas has a White Castle. Located outside the Best Western Casino Royale on the Strip, cravers can finally get what they need. No flight required.

White Castle Las Vegas
3411 Las Vegas Boulevard S., Las Vegas, 702-227-8531
whitecastlevegas.com

TIP
Miss other eating spots from back home? There's a Shake Shack at New York-New York and plenty of Raising Cane's and In-n-Out locations all over town.

TRY SOME TACOS
DOWNTOWN

Tacos are everywhere these days, but there are three spots on the fringes of downtown Las Vegas that are worth the trip out of the bright lights. Two are in the same shopping center, and the third serves tacos right out of a food truck in a tire shop parking lot. No frills, just flavor. If tacos aren't enough, you can always go for a burrito or torta.

Los Tacos, 1710 E Charleston Blvd., Las Vegas, 702-471-7447
lostacoslv.com

Tacos El Gordo, 1724 E Charleston Blvd., Las Vegas, 702-251-8226
tacoselgordobc.com

Taqueria El Buen Pastor food truck
503 Las Vegas Boulevard N., Las Vegas, 702-325-4020
taqueriaelbuenpastor.com

TIP
Adobada (spiced pork) is always a sure bet, but to
try different kinds of meat, choose from lengua (beef tongue),
buche (pork stomach), or sesos (beef brains).

MUSIC AND ENTERTAINMENT

YES, YOU CAN
GAMBLE HERE

Let's get this over with: There are plenty of places to gamble here. Whether you're deplaning, strolling through a resort, or dropping in to a convenience store or supermarket, you'll be greeted by slot machines. They've got every theme you could imagine: Wheel of Fortune, The Walking Dead, even Dolly Parton.

If you prefer interacting with dealers and other patrons, head to the casino floor for table games like poker, blackjack, craps, roulette, and baccarat. You can also try your luck at sports betting and put some money down on your favorite college or pro team or auto racing.

Just don't expect scratch-off tickets. Nevada makes you go across state lines for that. The closest thing you'll get to that is keno.

GLOBE-TROT
ON THE STRIP

Go ahead and accept one thing about the Strip: it's kitschy. Now with your mind right, be charmed on a mini-globe trot that's only a mile-and-a-half long. Ascend the half-sized Eiffel Tower at Paris Las Vegas, enjoying 360-degree views from forty-six stories up. Next check out Sin City's take on the Big Apple. New York-New York is rife with photo ops with replicas of the Statue of Liberty, Brooklyn Bridge, and the Manhattan skyline. For the last stop, head for the sphinxes guarding the huge pyramid called Luxor, named for the former Egyptian capital. Go at night to get a glimpse of its Sky Beam, which an astronaut said could be seen from space.

Paris Las Vegas, 3655 Las Vegas Boulevard S., Las Vegas, 702-946-7000
caesars.com/paris-las-vegas

New York-New York
3790 Las Vegas Boulevard S., Las Vegas, 702-740-6969
newyorknewyork.com

Luxor, 3900 Las Vegas Boulevard S., Las Vegas, 702-262-4000
luxor.com

TAKE IN SOME JAZZ
AT A FREE, OUTDOOR SHOW

Each May and June, some of the big names in jazz come to Las Vegas for a series of outdoor shows. And they're free. "Jazz in the Park" is a partnership between the Clark County government, the Las Vegas Jazz Society, and many sponsors. Some artists who've stopped by recently include Selina Albright, Marc Antoine, and the Brubeck Brothers Quartet. Bring low-back chairs or blankets to sit in the amphitheater at the Clark County Government Center. You can bring a picnic if you like, but food and drink vendors will be there if you'd rather let someone else do the work. Showtime is usually 7 p.m., but seats can fill up. And since you're just getting into summertime at this point, it will cool a bit after sundown.

Amphitheater at Clark County Government Center
500 S Grand Central Parkway, Las Vegas, 702-455-8200
(Clark County Parks and Recreation)
clarkcountynv.gov/depts/parks/Pages/jazz-inthe-park.aspx

SMOKE A CIGAR
AT NAPOLEON'S

Inside the Paris Hotel is Napoleon's Piano Bar. Now forget that side completely and head to the far right side of the joint, where you'll find a nice cigar lounge fit for smoking it up on special occasions. You can bring your own or buy a cigar there if you prefer. The atmosphere is perfect for sharing a smoke with loved ones or new friends, and a full menu of cognacs and other libations round out the experience. Ladies, this is the perfect Vegas father-daughter day, provided you're both over twenty-one.

Napoleon's Dueling Piano Bar
3655 S Las Vegas Blvd., Las Vegas, 702-946-7000

FEEL THE BEAT
OF AN EDM DEEJAY

The '70s had disco. The '90s had grunge. By the mid-aughts, electronic dance music was on the rise. Today, EDM is in, and there's no place that showcases it like Las Vegas. Some of the biggest deejays on the scene—Skrillex, David Guetta, Calvin Harris, Steve Aoki, and Tiesto—are regularly on the bill at nightclubs up and down the Strip. You'll likely have to pay and stand in long lines to see them, but once inside it's bound to be a pulsating, interesting time.

Hakkasan at MGM Grand
3799 Las Vegas Boulevard S., Las Vegas, 702-891-3838
hakkasanlv.com

XS Nightclub at Wynn Las Vegas
3131 Las Vegas Boulevard S., Las Vegas, 702-770-0097
xslasvegas.com

Drai's Beach Club at The Cromwell
3595 Las Vegas Boulevard S., Las Vegas, 702-737-0555
www.draislv.com

PLAY MINI GOLF
THE KISS WAY

While in Vegas, you must play the KISS by Monster Mini Golf course. Whether you're a hardcore KISS fan or a casual listener, you'd be hard pressed not to enjoy a round on these greens. KISS memorabilia abounds at the themed putt-putt course, and an onsite gift shop is stocked with every souvenir you'd need to remember the occasion. The golfing itself is an indoor, fun-filled adventure lit with black lights. The venue is also home to an arcade and bar, for a little extra fun, as if the KISS theme wasn't unique enough. Oh yeah, and you can get married at the onsite wedding chapel.

KISS by Monster Mini Golf
Rio All-Suite Hotel & Casino (Opening Spring 2016)
monsterminigolf.com/kiss

TIP
If you want more serious putting practice, consider a summertime trip to Angel Park. The putting course is lighted at night. For longer play, consider its walkable Cloud 9 course.
angelpark.com

DANCE
WITH THE BELLAGIO FOUNTAINS

Yes, it's just water and music and lights. But the combination makes the Fountains of Bellagio a captivating experience—ranked the number-one landmark in the United States. Choreographed jets of water shoot up to 420 feet skyward as they dance to music ranging from Madonna to EDM deejay Tiesto to Bruno Mars. Shows generally start every thirty minutes during the afternoon, and every fifteen minutes from the evening to midnight. Plus, the show is free.

Fountains of Bellagio
3600 Las Vegas Boulevard S., Las Vegas, 888-987-6667
bellagio.com/en/entertainment/fountains-of-bellagio.html

TIP
If you like Christmas music, definitely see the fountain in December. And remember, you dance with the music. Don't try to swim with it.

SPOT ALMOST ANY STAR
ALMOST ANYTIME

Celebrities love to perform and play—literally—in Las Vegas. While here, they can often pick up a corporate gig, indulge in a little entertainment themselves, or relax in world-class amenities while not onstage. It makes sense then, that if you want to see a comedian or musician, at some point, they'll probably show up. Artists such as Celine Dion, Elton John, Rod Stewart, and the trio of Reba and Brooks & Dunn hold residencies in Las Vegas. Others, such as Bruno Mars, Toby Keith, and Kid Rock, come out for shows fairly often. Comedians regularly grace Vegas stages, from Daniel Tosh and Jerry Seinfeld to Whitney Cummings and Lisa Lampanelli. While here, make sure to check out who's in town. And don't forget to keep your eyes peeled while walking the Strip or casino floors. You won't be disappointed.

TRACE VEGAS HISTORY
THROUGH THE NEON MUSEUM

There's no place that takes you back to the Vegas of yore like the Neon Museum. Sporting donated and loaned signs from operating casinos and those that have passed into the Neon Boneyard, this spot on the northern edge of downtown has old, glowing signs from the 1930s to now. Look for names like Caesars Palace, the Palms, and O'Shea's. Because this is valuable Vegas property, you must have a guided tour, and spots are limited. Call ahead or reserve early online.

Neon Museum
770 Las Vegas Boulevard N., Las Vegas, 702-387-6366
neonmuseum.org

DOWNTOWN MUSEUM TOUR

Within just a few miles of the Neon Museum are a handful of other historical sites that can be both fun and eye-opening. You can learn about Las Vegas' historical connection to the mafia or its Mormon pioneer heritage. Then let your kids learn about eco-friendly cities at a place just for them, or check out exhibits on dinosaurs and fossils at a Smithsonian-affiliated institution.

Mob Museum
300 Stewart Ave., Las Vegas, 702-229-2734
themobmuseum.org

Old Las Vegas Mormon Fort State Historic Park
500 E Washington Ave., Las Vegas, 702-486-3511
parks.nv.gov/parks/old-las-vegas-mormon-fort/

DISCOVERY Children's Museum
360 Promenade Place, Las Vegas, 702-382-5437
discoverykidslv.org

Las Vegas Natural History Museum
900 Las Vegas Boulevard N., Las Vegas, 702-384–3466
lvnhm.org

FULFILL
YOUR FREE-TIME DREAMS

Even when don't have a specific agenda in mind, Las Vegas can be whatever you want it to be. Practicing your hobby or enjoying your passion is possible here because of the many types of personalities the city attracts. Want to take a dance class from a world-class instructor? Pick your style. Feel like learning a magic trick? Done. If cooking is more your thing, check out cooking classes offered at some of the city's best restaurants. Want to learn a new song on the drums or guitar? Just book a lesson with a professional musician. Really, with all the performers who call Las Vegas home, you can find an expert in almost any type of hobby that interests you—you just have to look.

COWBOY UP
AT THE NATIONAL FINALS RODEO

You don't have to be a cowboy to go to the rodeo. Las Vegas has been home to the ten-day National Finals Rodeo for three decades. Generally in early- to mid-December, the event brings in tens of thousands of spectators to see the nation's best bull riding, steer wrestling, and tie-down roping. And if you want to pick up some new boots, spurs, or Western-themed jewelry, check out Cowboy Christmas. The bazaar takes up a convention hall.

National Finals Rodeo
Ticket information 702-260-8605
nfrexperience.com

TIP
Don't want to wait till December to get your cowboy on?
Take some free line dancing lessons at Gilley's at Treasure Island.
gilleyslasvegas.com

GEEK OUT
AT THE PINBALL HALL OF FAME

So you want to drop some money in a machine but have a clear idea of what you'll get back? The Pinball Hall of Fame will let you do that, and all games cost a quarter or fifty cents. With wooden machines from the 1950s to computer-chipped contraptions built in the 1990s, the whole family can play right through five decades of gaming history. There's a basketball-themed game named for Shaquille O'Neal, and others that will appeal to fans of Popeye, Monopoly, Star Wars, and Star Trek. At 10,000 square feet, the Las Vegas Pinball Collectors Club bills its place as the world's largest pinball collection.

Pinball Hall of Fame
1610 E Tropicana Ave., Las Vegas, 702-597-2627
pinballmuseum.org

TIP
Take an up-close look inside the Pinball Hall of Fame on Google Maps. It's one of the businesses that will allow you a 3D tour.

BE WOWED
BY THE WORLD'S TOP ACROBATS AND DANCERS

Earning a spot in a show on the Strip means you've got to have serious talent—and in most cases strength, balance, and flexibility. Cirque du Soleil offers eight shows that range from otherworldly to sexy to those with choreography that interprets the Beatles and Michael Jackson. Absinthe serves up acrobatics with off-color humor for those eighteen and over. Jabbawockeez has been praised for its hip-hop moves and family-friendly appeal.

Cirque du Soleil Las Vegas
cirquedusoleil.com/las-vegas

Absinthe at Caesars Palace
3570 Las Vegas Boulevard S., Las Vegas, 702-785-5395
absinthevegas.com

Jabbawockeez at the MGM Grand
3799 Las Vegas Boulevard S., Las Vegas, 702-531-3826
mgmgrand.com/en/entertainment/jabbawockeez.html

TIP
Nevada residents can get tickets at a discounted price. Tourists can also get cheaper tickets if they're part of a dinner or hotel package. Theaters want to fill seats, so you might be able to negotiate a better deal closer to showtime.

PREP
FOR THE ZOMBIE APOCALYPSE

Fans of the zombie genre will have plenty to work with in Las Vegas, from undead-themed stage shows to specialty stores and even a zombie shooting experience.

Zombie Burlesque at Planet Hollywood
3667 Las Vegas Boulevard S., Las Vegas, 866-932-1818
zombieburlesqueshow.com

Evil Dead The Musical at Tommy Wind Theater
3765 Las Vegas Boulevard S., Las Vegas, 702-895-9787
evildeadvegas.com

Zombie Apocalypse Store
3420 W Spring Mountain Rd., Las Vegas, 702-320-0703
zombieapocalypsestore.com

VIEW THE VALLEY
FROM ATOP A PERCH

The Strip and surrounding mountains can look impressive from just about any vantage point. But if you're lucky enough, the best view is from up high. Here are three spots to take in the Las Vegas Valley with a drink and music. These spots are adults only. That can mean a dress code, so call ahead.

Ghostbar, 55th floor at The Palms Casino Resort, with deck
4321 W Flamingo Rd., Las Vegas, 702-942-6832
palms.com/nightlife/ghostbar

The Mandarin Bar, 23rd floor at the Mandarin Oriental, inside
3752 Las Vegas Boulevard S., Las Vegas, 702-590-8888
mandarinoriental.com/lasvegas/fine-dining/mandarin-bar

The Foundation Room, 43rd floor at Mandalay Bay, with deck
3950 Las Vegas Boulevard S., Las Vegas, 702-632-7631
houseofblues.com/lasvegas/fr

TIP
For a truly moving, all-ages experience, check out the High Roller, a 550-foot-tall observation wheel. One go-round takes at least thirty minutes, and prices start at $25 a ride.
caesars.com/linq/high-roller

TAKE A GONDOLA RIDE
AT THE VENETIAN

It doesn't matter whether you understand Italian. What could be more romantic than riding in a flat-bottomed boat with a multitasking master who can steer the vessel, answer trivia questions about the resort, and sing an Italian ballad? Gondola rides are a fun and memorable way to experience The Venetian. Rides start at $21 per person.

3355 Las Vegas Boulevard S., Las Vegas, 702-414-4300
venetian.com/hotel/attractions/gondola-rides.html

GO TO A CONCERT

Las Vegas has lots of options when it comes to music. You can see a residency—the term used for artists who have an ongoing show at a casino—or catch a tour as it passes through. The valley also plays host to multiple huge festivals, regardless of the time of year. There are way too many musicians and venues to list here, but don't forget to check local music calendars whether you're planning a trip or you're a local. Here are a few events and venues to consider.

The Bunkhouse Saloon, 124 S 11th St., Las Vegas, 702-854-1414
bunkhousedowntown.com

Brooklyn Bowl, 3545 S Las Vegas Blvd., Las Vegas, 702-862-2695
brooklynbowl.com/las-vegas

The Pearl at Palms Casino Resort
4321 W Flamingo Rd., Las Vegas, 702-942-7777
palms.com/pearl-theater.html

Life is Beautiful
lifeisbeautiful.com

EDC
electricdaisycarnival.com

FIND FREE FUN
ON THE STRIP

Not much is free these days, but here are three attractions on the Strip that won't cost you anything but time.

Volcano at The Mirage

As volcanoes go, this one is erupting less frequently with age. It used to spew its fake lava from dusk until midnight. These days, it's once at 7 p.m. and 8 p.m. Sunday through Thursday with an additional show at 9 p.m. Fridays and Saturdays.

The Mirage, 3400 Las Vegas Boulevard S., Las Vegas
mirage.com/en/amenities/volcano.html

Conservatory and Botanical Garden at the Bellagio

Regardless of the time of year, you'll find something beautiful and enchanting here. Start by walking through the hotel lobby under artist Dale Chihuly's glass flowers that lead you to the real thing: a 14,000-square-foot indoor garden. Its plants change by the season, with a special installation for Chinese New Year.

Bellagio Hotel and Casino
3600 Las Vegas Boulevard S., Las Vegas
bellagio.com/en/entertainment/conservatory-botanical-garden.html

P3Studio at The Cosmopolitan

An artist-in-residence program that promotes interactivity. Sometimes it's spoken word, and artists need you to talk. Other times it will be painting or sculpting and you get an up-close view. It's easy to spot: the artists will be the people on the third floor making something interesting behind glass walls.

The Cosmopolitan of Las Vegas
3708 Las Vegas Boulevard S., Las Vegas
cosmopolitanlasvegas.com/experience/art.aspx

TIP

Fremont Street has free, outdoor concerts from local bands year-round. But summer brings national touring acts in the Rock of Vegas series. In the last few years, many of the shows have leaned toward '90s favorites including Spin Doctors, Everclear, Live, Toad the Wet Sprocket, Soul Asylum, and Eve 6.

SEE EXOTIC ANIMALS

Las Vegas doesn't have a typical zoo per se, but there are places in the city and nearby to see and sometimes pet animals you probably shouldn't keep as pets.

The Wildlife Habitat at the Flamingo

This free attraction includes exotic birds, reptiles, and fish. Appropriately, the exhibit includes the property's namesake pink flamingo.

3555 Las Vegas Boulevard S., Las Vegas, 702-733-3349
caesars.com/flamingo-las-vegas/things-to-do/wildlife-habitat

Roos-n-More Zoo

Head to this small-town attraction with lots of open space and more than three hundred animals, including camels, sloths, and kangaroos. Some petting is allowed under supervision. It's about fifty miles northeast of Las Vegas.

746 Snowden Ranch Rd., Moapa, 702-467-3585
roosnmore.org

The Lion Habitat Ranch

It's mainly the big cats here. This six-acre spot started as a retirement home for lions that lived at a now-closed MGM Grand habitat. Now there are a few ostriches and emus after another facility closed.

382 Bruner Ave., Henderson, 702-595-6666
lionhabitatranch.com

Siegfried & Roy's Secret Garden and Dolphin Habitat

This one is the father of all animal experiences in Las Vegas, as its namesakes helped put white tigers and Vegas on the map. Here you'll see white tigers, lions, leopards, and bottlenose dolphins.

Inside The Mirage, 3400 Las Vegas Boulevard S., Las Vegas
800-374-9000
mirage.com

Bonnie Springs Restaurant and Bar

Llamas, wolves, and a lynx are some of the main attractions in the zoo at this small, Western-themed resort. Adults can ride horses and kids can ride ponies that all make their homes in the stables. There are farm animals in the petting section.

16935 Bonnie Springs Rd., Las Vegas
702-875-4191
bonniesprings.com

TIP

Punxsutawney has Phil the groundhog. Las Vegas has Mojave Max the desert tortoise. Kids can enter a contest to pick when they think he'll wake up for the start of spring. See him at the visitor center at Red Rock Canyon National Conservation Area.
mojavemax.com

SPORTS AND RECREATION

WALK
THE FREMONT STREET EXPERIENCE

It might be one of the oldest parts of town, but this five-block stretch doesn't act its age. The Fremont Street Experience—a pedestrian mall shaded by a fifteen-hundred-foot-long screen built from 12.5 million LED lights—is open twenty-four hours. It's lined by casinos, gift shops, restaurants, and bars. Viva Vision, the overhead screen that fire lighted up in 1995, plays music videos. And in the summer there are free concerts along the route.

Las Vegas doesn't have many acts featuring showgirls these days, but you might spot a few women and sometimes men dressed in sparkly bikinis and feathered hats along Fremont. Buskers, as they're known, dress up so you'll take photos with them—and they expect a tip. If you strike a pose, be prepared to give them some cash. You'll see costumes ranging from superheros to brides to silver-painted statues. Parents should be aware that some of the costumes show lots of skin.

Fremont Street Experience
between Main Street and Las Vegas Boulevard
vegasexperience.com

TIP
Adults are allowed to carry their alcoholic beverages in plastic cups only. Opening packaged liquor is illegal. If you have questions, just ask your server or store clerk.

RIDE
THE RED ROCK SCENIC LOOP

It would be a shame to see Las Vegas but never take in its surrounding natural beauty. The easiest way to do that is by riding the 13.1-mile scenic drive at Red Rock Canyon National Conservation Area. There are parking spots along the way, so you can stop for a photo or take a hike. (Camping is available with a permit.) You'll see an amazing array of rock formations—some jagged, some smooth, and some a deep pink or red—while climbing to heights of seven thousand feet above sea level. From some vantage points, you can see the Strip, which is twenty miles away. It's a popular route for cyclists, so go the speed limit. Look for climbers as you pass the cliffs—they'll be tiny compared to the rock faces they're tackling.

More Red Rocks
It's a little further out of town (fifty miles northeast), but Valley of Fire State Park is less crowded and worth the drive. Look for the appropriately named Elephant Rock arch just off the road near the park's east entrance.

Valley of Fire State Park
29450 Valley of Fire Rd., Moapa Valley, NV 89040
702-397-2088
parks.nv.gov/parks/valley-of-fire-state-park/

DISCOVER A DESERT OASIS:
CLARK COUNTY WETLANDS PARK

You won't find a lazy river, but the biggest park in Clark County still provides plenty of fun.

The Wetlands Park offers something unexpected for the desert: streams and ponds. As expected for Las Vegas, they aren't exactly natural. They come from runoff and reclaimed water that eventually make their way to Lake Mead.

Before they get there, they form a twenty-nine-hundred-acre oasis that makes a habitat for trees and reeds, birds and bunnies, and even . . . mosquitoes. It makes a great place for humans to view and photograph wildlife or take a stroll or bicycle ride. Best of all, admission is free. Open 9 a.m. to 3 p.m. daily.

Clark County Wetlands Park
7050 E Wetlands Park Lane, Las Vegas, 702-455-7522
clarkcountynv.gov/wetlandspark

POUND THE PAVEMENT
FOR A VIP VIEW OF
LAS VEGAS BOULEVARD

Most marathoners are used to being up before sunrise the day of the big race. But like most things Las Vegas, the stop on the Rock 'n' Roll Marathon circuit is built for a later schedule.

Here, the race starts just after sundown to offer views of The Strip in all its glory. Las Vegas Boulevard is closed to vehicles, and thirty-five thousand walkers, joggers, and runners take off down the spine of the Strip.

If 26.2 miles seems a bit of a stretch, event organizers offer shorter distances: a half-marathon, 10K, and 5K. Keeping with the race series' musical theme, bands jam along the route, and a big act plays a sendoff set before the pavement gets pounded. In 2014, the year they picked up four Grammy Awards, Macklemore & Ryan Lewis played the pre-race show.

Las Vegas Rock 'n' Roll Marathon, Half Marathons and 5K Races
runrocknroll.com/las-vegas/

CATCH A GAME
(AND MAYBE A BASEBALL)
AT A 51s GAME

Why a metro area with a population of more than two million doesn't have major league professional sports is at the center of an ongoing debate. But while the politicians, millionaires, and casinos work that out, you can enjoy a little pro baseball at minor league prices.

Named for the classified area north of Las Vegas where many believe the federal government keeps all its secrets about aliens, the 51s play at the City of Las Vegas-owned Cashman Field. The team, previously known as the Stars, is part of the AAA Pacific Coast League and is an affiliate of the New York Mets.

Tickets start at $10 and often come with a bonus for the first twenty-five hundred or so through the gate: branded playing cards, sun shades, or pint glasses. There's often a fireworks show at the end.

Cashman Field
850 Las Vegas Boulevard N., Las Vegas, lasvegas.51s.milb.com

PONDER
THE PRICKLY JOSHUA TREE

One of the Mojave Desert's main mascots is a plant whose leaves look like a porcupine. Green barbs top the twisted branches of the Joshua tree, and after the spikes die, they form a shaggy skirt down the trunk.

Native Americans used pieces of this fibrous plant to make baskets and shoes. But it was Mormon settlers who christened it with its common name, honoring Old Testament figure Joshua. To them, the branches looked like hands stretched toward heaven. Rock band U2 titled its 1987 album after this member of the agave family. And there's a national park named for it in Southern California. The Park Service describes it as "straight out of a Dr. Seuss book."

To find Joshua trees in the wild, look anywhere along I-15 heading into Las Vegas from the north or south. For a closer view, visit Red Rock Canyon National Conservation Area or the Botanical Cactus Garden at Ethel M Chocolates.

Red Rock Canyon National Conservation Area
1000 Scenic Loop Dr., Las Vegas, 702-515-5350
redrockcanyonlv.org

Ethel M Chocolates
2 Cactus Garden Dr., Henderson, 800-438-4356
ethelm.com

BE WOWED BY
NEARBY NATIONAL PARKS

Three of the finest national parks in the Southwest are just a hop, skip and a jump away from Las Vegas. Just remember that out West you take bigger strides. You can be at the gates of any of these beauties in two-and-a-half hours or less and still make Las Vegas your basecamp.

Lake Mead National Recreation Area
Nevada/Arizona line
The main visitors' center is off U.S. Highway 93 south of Boulder City, Nevada, about 30 miles south of Las Vegas
702-293-8906, nps.gov/lake

Zion National Park, Springdale, Utah
About 160 miles and two-and-a-half hours northeast of Las Vegas via I-15
Visitor information 435-772-3256
nps.gov/zion

Death Valley National Park
California/Nevada line
About 120 miles and 2 hours northwest of Las Vegas via State Route 160
Visitor information 760-786-3200
nps.gov/deva

SAFETY TIPS

Remember, this is the desert. These places are remote, so take your own water. If it happens to rain when you're in a low-lying area, get out. It doesn't take much to start a flash flood. In the summer, Death Valley and Lake Mead can get well above 110 degrees. They're much pleasanter in the winter.

GET A TASTE OF WINTER
ON MOUNT CHARLESTON

Postcards paint a picture of endless summer in Las Vegas. It's true that the valley gets close to five months of summertime temperatures. But it's a different story in the nearby Spring Mountains National Recreation Area. Locally referred to as Mount Charleston, the actual highest point in the range at 11,916 feet, this section of Humboldt-Toiyabe National Forest is generally about twenty degrees cooler than the city. And it snows.

It snows enough to keep the folks that run the Las Vegas Ski and Snowboard Resort happy, even though they have machines to make it if Mother Nature doesn't come through. Price of lift tickets varies.

If sledding is more your style, families gather from December through early spring at Lee Meadows to slide down the hill on everything from real sleds to boogie boards and the occasional laundry basket. If you like snowshoeing, there are plenty of trails that will be covered in snow.

6725 Lee Canyon Rd., Las Vegas, 702-385-2754
skilasvegas.com/

SLIDE WITH THE SHARKS,
OR WATCH A MERMAID

Yes, they had to travel a long way to get here. But Las Vegas has plenty of exotic water creatures. Whether you booked a room to slide through a tube—safely—with sharks at the Golden Nugget or you showed up for the free mermaid performance at the Silverton, there's something fun for everybody's price range.

Shark Tank and Chute at the Golden Nugget
129 E Fremont St., Las Vegas, 702-385-7111
goldennugget.com/lasvegas/pool_thetank.asp

Shark Reef Aquarium at Mandalay Bay
3950 S Las Vegas Blvd., Las Vegas, 702-632-4555
sharkreef.com

Mermaid Aquarium at Silverton Hotel & Casino
3333 Blue Diamond Rd., Las Vegas, 702-263-7777
silvertoncasino.com/

FLY WITH THE BIRDS
ON A ZIP LINE

If staying on the ground isn't your thing, there's another exhilarating option for taking it all in: zip lines. Three Southern Nevada businesses can take you up in the air and zip you along your merry way. Rides range from $20 to $150-plus.

Slotzilla will send you flying over Fremont Street in downtown Las Vegas. Options include a lower, shorter ride in a sitting position or a higher, longer ride lying on your belly, Superman-style. Wave at the revelers below if you dare!

To get views of the Strip, try VooDoo ZipLine. On this ride you'll soar five hundred feet above the ground between two towers at the Carnival-inspired Rio. In the evenings, you must be twenty-one or older to ride.

For more a rugged experience, head out of town to Boulder City. Flightlinez Bootleg Canyon has separate legs of its zip lines, covering more than 1.5 miles in three hours. You'll be out of sight of the city, so enjoy the Mojave Desert beauty of the Red Mountains.

Slotzilla, 425 Fremont St., #160, Las Vegas, 702-678-5780
vegasexperience.com/slotzilla-zip-line

VooDoo ZipLine, Rio All-Suite Hotel and Casino
3700 W Flamingo Rd., Las Vegas, 866-746-7671, voodoozipline.com

Flightlinez Bootleg Canyon
1644 Nevada Highway (U.S. Highway 93), Boulder City, 702-293-6885
flightlinezbootleg.com

PICK YOUR OWN PRODUCE
AT GILCREASE ORCHARD

Farmland doesn't immediately come to mind when you think of the Mojave Desert. But Gilcrease Orchard in North Las Vegas was built around springs that made it a literal oasis. Some version has been around since the 1920s, and it's now run by a nonprofit foundation that allows residents and visitors to come pick everything from pears to pumpkins and eggplants to apples. Keep in mind that produce is seasonal, so call ahead if you're not clear about when your favorite fruits should be ripe.

7800 N Tenaya Way, Las Vegas, 702-409-0655
thegilcreaseorchard.org

TIP
Check around Christmastime, when the orchard offers hayrides and pictures with Santa.

HIKE YOUR WAY
TO HAPPINESS

Sometimes you just need to get out of town to seek some peace and quiet. You can find that solitude in as little as a thirty-minute drive outside Las Vegas. Whether it's jagged rock formations, trees (yes, trees) or desert dwelling creatures such as the bighorn sheep, there is beauty to behold. Here are three favorite trails. Each involves various levels of incline, so take note.

Bristlecone Trail at Mount Charleston

Getting to the trailhead: Take U.S. 95 north about thirty miles out of town, turn left onto Lee Canyon Road (state route 156) and go till it ends. You can park near the trailhead, which is marked.

Length: 6.2 miles one way

Features: Ancient bristlecone pines, aspens that shimmer yellow and orange in the fall.

mtcharlestonresort.com

Ice Box Canyon at Red Rock Canyon National Conservation Area

Getting to the trailhead: Take the scenic loop to mile marker 8. The marked trailhead will be on your right, with parking.

Length: 2.6 miles one way

Features: Plenty of shade and seasonal waterfalls.

redrockcanyonlv.org

Liberty Bell Arch Trail at Lake Mead National Recreation Area

Getting to the trailhead: Take U.S. 93 south. The trailhead (with a sign that says White Rock Canyon) is about 3.5 miles past Hoover Dam. Park there, and walk under the highway overpass to start the hike.

Length: 5.3 miles one way

Features: An arch that looks like the Liberty Bell, with an incredible overlook of the Colorado River.

alltrails.com

HIT THE TRAIL ON HORSEBACK

Seriously. Las Vegas has a few horseback trail ride companies that cater to the public, and the city's weather and scenery make the perfect backdrop for a relaxing trail ride. Just don't go in the middle of summer in the triple-digit heat. That wouldn't make for a very enjoyable experience. Otherwise, your trail ride will most likely wind through parts of Red Rock Canyon, where you can view the city's more serene side while getting a nice leg workout. It's a beautiful way to spend a couple of hours, and one of the more unexpected ways to play while in Las Vegas. Try out Cowboy Trail Rides, a longtime Las Vegas company.

Cowboy Trail Rides
4053 Fossil Ridge Rd., Las Vegas,
702-387-2457

CATCH A FISH
AT A LAS VEGAS PARK

No, no, they're not native. But Las Vegas-area parks are stocked, often with catfish and trout, and you're welcome to catch them. There are rules: If you are twelve or older, you need a state-issued fishing license, and there are limits on how many you can take with you, so do your research before casting a line.

Parks with ponds:

Floyd Lamb Park
9200 Tule Springs Rd., Las Vegas, 702-229-8100

Lorenzi Park
3343 W Washington Ave., Las Vegas, 702-229-6718

Sunset Park
2601 E Sunset Rd., Las Vegas, 702-455-8200

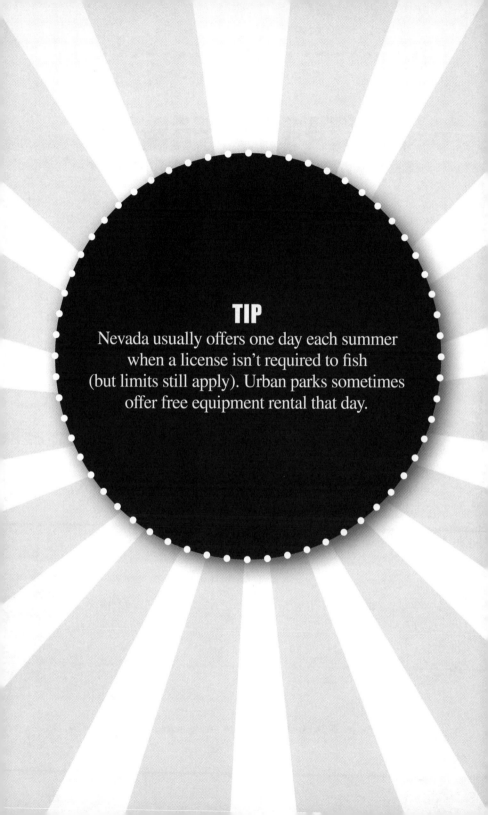

TIP

Nevada usually offers one day each summer when a license isn't required to fish (but limits still apply). Urban parks sometimes offer free equipment rental that day.

HUNT FOR TREASURE
THE MODERN WAY: GEOCACHING

One free, fun way to see the beautiful natural areas around all the glitz and glamour is to go geocaching in Southern Nevada. Being a desert, Las Vegas and its surrounding areas are ripe for desert adventurers to stow buried treasure, and geocaching is a popular pastime for those living in the region. From caches hidden at wedding chapels to those requiring an off-road drive to find them, new adventurers and more experienced geocachers will all find what they're looking for.

Many geocaching websites feature directions, coordinates, and tips in member posts, and if you've never been, we suggest reading up a bit on the hobby to learn the expected etiquette. Really, though, geocaching in the Las Vegas area is a great, free way to see the lay of the land. Check out www.geocaching.com for favorite Las Vegas sites and tips. Social sites such as YouTube also feature videos and users' experiences.

SHOOT
A MACHINE GUN—OR ANY OTHER NUMBER OF FIREARMS

While visiting Las Vegas, you may feel the need to do something exciting that perhaps you can't do where you live. If so, the city has multiple indoor gun ranges that allow visitors to shoot machine guns with the oversight of a qualified staff member. The granddaddy of these ranges, The Gun Store, offers multiple shooting packages tailored to customers' desires. Most of the ranges offer opportunities to shoot AR-15s, AK-47s, rifles, and handguns. Experiences can range from as tame to as lively as you want, from shooting zombies to simply practicing your aim.

The Gun Store
2900 E Tropicana Ave., Las Vegas, 702-454-1110
thegunstorelasvegas.com

Machine Guns Vegas
3501 Aldebaran Ave., Las Vegas, 800-757-4668
machinegunsvegas.com

Battlefield Vegas
2771 Industrial Rd., Las Vegas, 702-566-1000
battlefieldvegas.com

STARE UP AT AN AIRSHOW
AT NELLIS AIR FORCE BASE

Las Vegas' Nellis Air Force Base is home to the USAF Thunderbirds, an elite flying unit within the U.S. Air Force. Throughout the year the unit travels and performs air shows, but if you happen to be in Vegas when the Thunderbirds are in the sky, this is one show you shouldn't miss. The majestic planes fly in synchronicity at Nellis' air shows, and Las Vegas locals make a day of going out to see the pilots do their thing. Pack plenty of sunscreen and plan for the heat if going during spring or summer, and in winter or fall remember to take a coat. You'll primarily be outside for this one.

TIP
Want to learn about the history of flight in Las Vegas?
You can see it on your way in or out of town at the Howard W. Cannon
Aviation Museum at McCarran International Airport. The main
exhibit is on the second level, above baggage claim.
mccarran.com/Relax/AviationMuseum.aspx

ATTEND A SHOW
AT THE SMITH CENTER'S CABARET JAZZ

The Smith Center for the Performing Arts hosts Broadway shows on a regular basis. But the Smith Center also has a great room that can sometimes be overshadowed by its larger, more publicized sister. Cabaret Jazz is home to fantastic vocalists, living legends, and some of the best entertainment you can find in Las Vegas. The intimate room features cocktail tables for comfortable, albeit hip, seating, and attendees can order snacks, drinks, or dinner, depending on their hearts' desire. If you're looking for a fun night out with solid entertainers, check out Cabaret Jazz. You won't be disappointed.

Smith Center for the Performing Arts
361 Symphony Park Ave., Las Vegas, 702-749-2012
thesmithcenter.com/cabaretjazz/

SEE
A NATIONAL MONUMENT FOR FOSSILS

Most of Nevada—more than eighty percent—is controlled by the federal government. Most of it is pretty barren. But there's one place right outside Las Vegas that's fertile, at least with Ice Age fossils. Tule Springs Fossil Beds National Monument was designated in 2014. The 22,650-acre site, which is forty-three miles long, has yielded bones from mammoths, lions, and sloths. Some of the fossils are believed to be two hundred thousand years old. So the stuff that makes it special is ancient, but the designation, as government's pace goes, is new. There's no welcome center, parking lot, or facilities. The rules are to keep vehicles on paved roads, and everywhere else is open to hiking. There are no designated trails, so tread lightly. If you find a fossil, call the National Park Service.

Tule Springs Fossil Beds National Monument
Access points where 5th St., Decatur Blvd.
and Durango Drive end at the desert|
702-293-8922
nps.gov/tusk

TIP
If you don't want to hike to spot fossils, see them at the
Nevada State Museum at Springs Preserve,
or the Las Vegas Natural History Museum.

SNAP UP ORIGINAL ARTWORK
AT ART IN THE PARK IN BOULDER CITY

Each year on the first weekend of October, Boulder City hosts Art in the Park. About twenty minutes away from Las Vegas, the outdoor art festival is a nice drive away from the main action. Plan to spend the day in this charming enclave that sprang up when the Hoover Dam was built. The main drag and town square are lined with eateries, antique shops, and artist dens, and no gambling—it's banned. The actual festival takes place throughout the city's lush parks and is a fundraiser for the Boulder City Hospital Foundation. Attendance is a Las Vegas locals' tradition, and it's hard not to find at least one treasure to take home. For more information, visit bchcares.org/foundation/art-in-the-park.

Spots to stop on a Boulder City stroll

Boulder City/Hoover Dam Museum (in the Boulder Dam Hotel)
1305 Arizona St., Boulder City, 702-294-1988
bcmha.org

Milo's Inn at Boulder
534 Nevada Way, Boulder City, 702-294-4244
milosbouldercity.com

The Coffee Cup
512 Nevada Way, Boulder City, 702-294-0517
worldfamouscoffeecup.com

● ●

STROLL THE UNLV CAMPUS
IN THE SPRING OR FALL

Las Vegas' largest university, the University of Nevada, Las Vegas, is east of the Strip on Maryland Parkway. Venture over to this side of town, grab a bite to eat in the university district, then head over to the campus itself for a little walk. Throughout the school semesters, you'll get plenty of ambiance from the students themselves, but periodically there's art and other things to see when class is in session. Mature trees and wide-open walkways make a stroll around this college campus relaxing and a perfect place to take in some fresh air.

UNLV campus
4505 S Maryland Parkway, Las Vegas, 702-895-3011

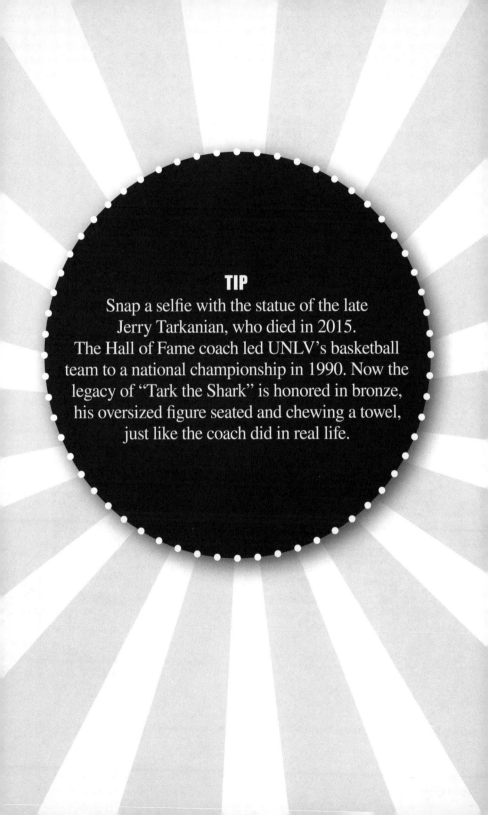

TIP

Snap a selfie with the statue of the late
Jerry Tarkanian, who died in 2015.
The Hall of Fame coach led UNLV's basketball
team to a national championship in 1990. Now the
legacy of "Tark the Shark" is honored in bronze,
his oversized figure seated and chewing a towel,
just like the coach did in real life.

RING IN
THE NEW YEAR

At least once, come to Las Vegas for New Year's Eve. It can be as grand or low-key as you make it. The streets are lined with revelers, most people are in a festive mood, and it can get a little nutty around midnight on Las Vegas Boulevard. Indoors, nightclubs, restaurants, and hotels provide high-end parties for those willing to fork over cash to sip champagne and have a front-row seat to the city's annual fireworks show. Outside, the aforementioned revelers provide plenty of entertainment for those wishing to forgo admission fees. Either way, it's a memorable party that everyone should experience. Check out the Las Vegas Convention and Visitors Authority's website for firework and citywide information: lasvegas.com.

TIP
There may not be snow, but New Year's Eve is still wintertime in Las Vegas. So be prepared for cold weather—temperatures are often in the 30s. If you stay outside, be sure to layer. To get inside many casinos, you have to have restaurant or room reservations.
Don't forget Fremont Street downtown hosts a party, too.

SIGN UP
FOR THE SLOT CLUB

If you like freebies and are going to gamble anyway, sign up for the casinos' slot clubs. The clubs track your play, usually on table games and slots, and will reward you for loyalty with items such as free buffets, free gifts, and invites to players-only parties. Sometimes, you'll receive a free gift just for signing up. If you're going to put money in the machines anyway, it's a good way to get a little extra back for playing. Sometimes the gifts are really nice, too, and you'll hear about fun events going on that may add a little something extra to your stay.

> **TIP**
> One way to make a loyalty program work is by asking for an upgrade. If the place isn't fully booked, the club may be able to help move you to one with a better view for a little or no extra charge. Remember, be nice with the ask. An upgrade is a courtesy.

EXPLORE
A GHOST TOWN

You don't have to get too far outside Las Vegas to find remnants of towns that have seen better days. But there are three well-preserved and accessible ghost towns that are worth exploring.

Goodsprings

The main draw in this former mining town is the Pioneer Saloon, still serving up drinks and entertainment more than one hundred years after it opened. The town still has a well-preserved schoolhouse and a cemetery with the oldest grave dating back to 1890. The Goodsprings Historical Society has lots more information.

Getting there: take I-15 south to exit 12. Hang a right on State Route 161 until you see the saloon. About forty miles southwest of Las Vegas.

goodsprings.org   pioneersaloon.info

Nelson

This old mining town is more of an artists' colony these days. It's a popular spot for high school senior portraits with old trucks, outhouses, and even a weathered piano. You can still get a glimpse of how life used to be on a paid tour of a shuttered gold mine. It's about a quarter of a mile, and takes about an hour.

Getting there: take U.S. Highway 95 south, and keep on it just before getting to Boulder City. Then take Nevada Highway 165 through beautiful El Dorado Canyon. About forty-five miles south of Las Vegas.

eldoradocanyonminetours.com

St. Thomas

This Mormon settlement that dates back to the 1860s was abandoned to make way for Lake Mead. It was once under at least sixty feet of water, but drought is driving down lake levels, and building foundations are surfacing. The water has receded enough for a walk through in some spots.

Getting there: from I-15, go through Valley of Fire State Park. Shortly after entering Lake Mead National Recreation Area, turn left onto Old Saint Thomas Road, and drive straight toward the lake. About sixty miles northeast of Las Vegas.

nps.gov/lake/learn/nature/st-thomas-nevada.htm

TIP
Drive past Nelson for great views of the Colorado River.
You can't see it anymore, but steamboats used to make their way
to an inland port here called Nelson's Landing.

HOLLER
FOR THE UNLV BASKETBALL TEAM

UNLV basketball fans are as loyal as boosters of any other program in the country. The games at the Thomas & Mack Center are lively and fun, and the fans are welcoming and passionate. Get yourself a black and red UNLV shirt for a souvenir, enjoy a cold beverage, and shout "Re-Bels" with the rest of the crowd. The Runnin' Rebels have seen their share of fame with a national championship, and tickets are affordable, making this a fun night out.

unlvtickets.com/athletics

TIP

During the summer, check out up-and-coming professional basketball players in the Thomas & Mack Center. The NBA Summer League showcases a mix of rookies and second-year players, and you can see multiple games for the price of one regular-season ticket.

nba.com/summerleague

SHOW OFF YOUR MOVES
IN A CASINO LOUNGE

Las Vegas lounges can hold the most fun you'll have in the city, if you play your cards right. On weekends especially, hotel lounges offer quality bands playing music from a variety of genres for free. During the National Finals Rodeo, many of the lounges offer country music to go along with citywide theming. While the bands are playing, many get up and dance, from ballroom dancers to those just looking to get down. Plus, you'll get to see some of the best musicians, who are often playing in the lounges. Most of the lounges are free, and an attached bar will offer plenty of seating for people-watching if that's more your thing.

Here are a few spots to try:

Eyecandy
Mandalay Bay, 3950 Las Vegas Blvd. S, Las Vegas, 702-632-7777
mandalaybay.com/en/nightlife/eyecandy-sound-lounge.html

The Lounge
Palms, 4321 W Flamingo Rd., Las Vegas, 702-942-7777
palms.com/the-lounge.html

South Padre
Texas Station, 2101 Texas Star Lane, North Las Vegas, 702-631-1000
texasstation.sclv.com/Entertainment/South-Padre.aspx

SKATE A LOOP
AROUND AN ICE RINK

Many Las Vegas ice skating rinks are seasonal, but if you really need to work on your axel, you can find some ice just about any time. The Las Vegas Ice Center, on the western side of town, is open year-round, but with specials during the winter. At least two rinks usually pop up around the holidays: in Downtown Summerlin and at the Cosmopolitan. Expect cold-weather classics like hot chocolate, s'mores and maybe even Santa in December.

Las Vegas Ice Center
9295 W Flamingo Rd., Las Vegas, 702-320-7777
lasvegasice.com

Rock Rink at Downtown Summerlin
1980 Festival Plaza Dr., Las Vegas, 702-832-1000
downtownsummerlin.com/eventscalendar

Ice Rink at the Cosmopolitan
The Cosmopolitan of Las Vegas
3708 Las Vegas Boulevard S., Las Vegas, 702-698-7000
cosmopolitanlasvegas.com/experience/icerink.aspx

HAVE A NEW YORK CITY DATE NIGHT
WITHOUT LEAVING THE STRIP

Work up an appetite playing inside the New York-New York Hotel's arcade, then get an adrenaline rush from a ride on The Big Apple Coaster, which features a 180-degree heartline twist. Like many other venues in the city, you can even get hitched aboard the red rollercoaster. After you've had your thrills, head to the property's onsite Nathan's Famous Hot Dogs to get a taste of Coney Island's finest. If you find yourself needing some air after your arcade-rollercoaster adventure, take a short jaunt to Bobby's Burger Palace, a Las Vegas outpost of New York City chef Bobby Flay's famed burger joint. There, Flay serves up gourmet burgers, alcohol-infused milkshakes, and plenty of sides.

New York-New York Hotel & Casino
3790 S Las Vegas Blvd., Las Vegas, 702-740-6969
newyorknewyork.com

Bobby's Burger Palace
3750 S Las Vegas Blvd., Las Vegas, 702-598-0191
bobbysburgerpalace.com

SAVOR
AN ARTISAN COCKTAIL

Las Vegas is loaded with talented bartenders, and some of them are just downright artists. At many higher-end casino or nightclub bars, patrons can order specialty cocktails from seasonal menus. Try an infused libation at Aria's Lobby Bar, or have a classic cocktail at Bellagio's Petrossian Bar. The latter even offers an afternoon tea, if you're looking for a warmup before cocktail hour. Other places to order an artisan drink in Las Vegas include the Chandelier bar at The Cosmopolitan and Parasol Up at Wynn Las Vegas. Be sure to ask for a menu at each to see what's being offered during your stay.

Aria
3730 Las Vegas Boulevard S., Las Vegas, 702-590-7111
aria.com

Bellagio
3600 Las Vegas Boulevard S., Las Vegas, 702-693-7111
bellagio.com

The Cosmopolitan
3708 Las Vegas Boulevard S., Las Vegas, 702-698-7000
cosmopolitanlasvegas.com

Wynn Las Vegas
3131 Las Vegas Boulevard S., Las Vegas, 702-770-7000
wynnlasvegas.com

WATCH
A TRIBUTE SHOW

One thing Las Vegas does well and has done for years is put on a great tribute. From its tribute-based hotel properties to the shows themselves, Vegas does imitation as a form of flattery right. While here, you should absolutely go see one of the city's premier impersonator shows. There's Divas, led by Vegas royalty Frank Marino, and of course the famous Legends in Concert, which features a rotating cast impersonating icons such as Madonna, Britney, and Elvis. Other shows feature country superstars, a Motown-style revue with a side of Tina Turner and Aretha Franklin, the Rat Pack, The Beatles, and other famous acts you just might not otherwise get to see in concert.

Divas
Performing at the LINQ
3535 S Las Vegas Blvd., Las Vegas, 702-731-3311
divas.vegas

Legends in Concert
Performing at the Flamingo
3555 S Las Vegas Blvd., Las Vegas, 702-777-2782
legendsinconcert.com/las-vegas

The Rat Pack is Back
Performing at The Tuscany Suites
255 E Flamingo Rd., Las Vegas, 702-947-5781
ratpackisback.com

Country Superstars
Performing at Bally's
3645 Las Vegas Boulevard S., Las Vegas, 877-603-4390
caesars.com

Hitzville The Show
Performing at Planet Hollywood
3667 Las Vegas Blvd., Las Vegas, 702-260-7200
hitzvilletheshow.com

COOL OFF
IN A POOL OR THE WILDERNESS

If you're outdoors in Southern Nevada in the summer, you're going to want to get in the water. From May to September, the high temperatures will regularly top one hundred degrees, and sometimes the mercury will push 115. Never fear, you have options.

Nearly every hotel on the Strip has a pool. Do your research to figure out whether you want a place to read a book or take the kids or if you want a dayclub—a deejay and a pool packed with people dancing in their bathing suits. (Some are even toptional.) The Las Vegas Valley also has two water parks, where you can swim and slide to your heart's desire.

If you're looking for a more remote experience, you could float or paddle down the Colorado River, south of Hoover Dam and thirty miles or more outside Las Vegas, depending on how far you go. You're welcome to take your own boat or tubes, rent from an outfitter, or get a guided tour.

WATER PARKS

Cowabunga Bay
900 Galleria Dr., Henderson, 702-850-9000
cowabungabayvegas.com

Wet'n'Wild Las Vegas
7055 S Fort Apache Rd., Las Vegas, 702-979-1600
wetnwildlasvegas.com

KAYAK, CANOE RENTALS, AND GUIDES

Desert Adventures
1647-A Nevada Highway, Boulder City, 702-293-5026
kayaklasvegas.com

Black Canyon/Willow Beach River Adventures
P.O. Box 60130, Boulder City, 800-455-3490
blackcanyonadventures.com

CULTURE AND HISTORY

SAY "CHEESE"
AT THE WELCOME TO LAS VEGAS SIGN

If anything is iconic in Las Vegas, it's this flashing neon greeting at the south end of the Strip. Constructed in 1959 by the Clark County Commission—the governing body for the county, because the Strip is actually outside the Las Vegas city limits—it's been one of the few structures in this four-mile stretch of Las Vegas Boulevard that hasn't changed in an otherwise dynamic half century (other than going solar a few years back). It's a testimony to its designer, Clark County native Betty Willis, who died at 91 in 2015. The "Welcome To Fabulous Las Vegas Nevada" sign was listed on the National Register of Historic Places in 2009.

"Welcome To Fabulous Las Vegas Nevada" sign
In the median, a half-mile south of the intersection of
Las Vegas Blvd. and Russell Rd.

TIP
You can drive or walk to the sign. There are a few dozen parking spots, and the county recently put in a new traffic signal for pedestrians. Still, look both ways before you cross the street.

CELEBRATE HISPANIC CULTURE
IN LAS VEGAS

The Hispanic Museum of Nevada works to make the region's Latin and Caribbean influences accessible to all. Its offerings include sculptures, photographs, paintings, and pottery, plus the organization puts on the Latino Film Festival. It also serves as an event space for local groups to host parties. A 2015 party encouraged attendees to paste on a unibrow or mustache in honor of Frida Kahlo and Salvador Dali in celebration of eccentric and interesting personalities. The museum also has an exhibit called "MTV Pop Culture Wall," which includes signatures of artists who signed on the now-canceled show *Total Request Live*. Entertainers who signed include Christina Aguilera, Jay Z, Carmen Electra, and Kanye West.

Hispanic Museum of Nevada at The Boulevard Mall
3680 S Maryland Parkway, Las Vegas, 702-773-2203
hispanicmuseumnv.com

FIND SANCTUARY
AT SPRINGS PRESERVE

When Spanish-speaking explorers seeking a new route from New Mexico to California passed through Southern Nevada in the late 1820s, a view of the valley revealed springs and lush grass. It was christened Las Vegas, which translates to "the meadows."

Most of the springs have gone dry. But to get a glimpse of what Las Vegas used to look like, check out the 180-acre Springs Preserve. The Las Vegas Valley Water Authority-owned conservation area includes interpretive trails, botanical gardens, and museums with exhibits on sustainable water use. Listed on the National Register of Historic Places, it's also home to outdoor concerts and family-friendly festivals year round.

Springs Preserve
333 S Valley View Blvd., Las Vegas, 702-822-7700
springspreserve.org

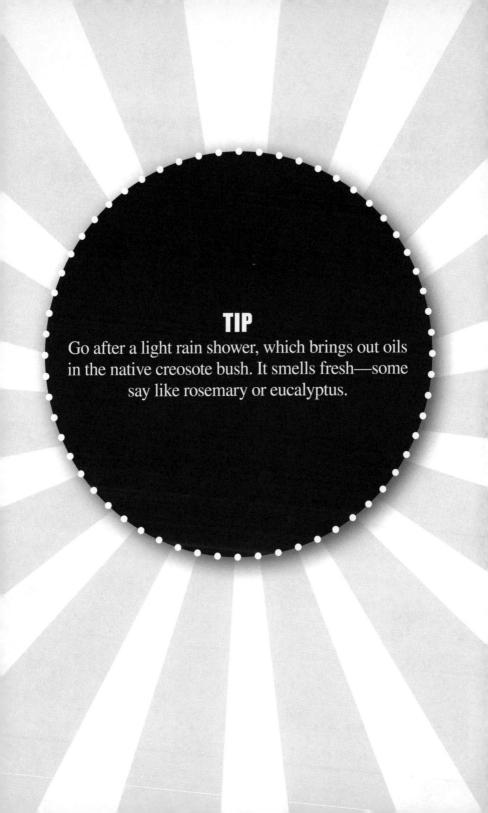

TIP
Go after a light rain shower, which brings out oils in the native creosote bush. It smells fresh—some say like rosemary or eucalyptus.

STRADDLE TWO STATES
AND TWO TIME ZONES AT HOOVER DAM

Forty-five minutes outside Las Vegas lies Hoover Dam. Completed in 1936, the concrete structure towers 726 feet above the Colorado River to form Lake Mead. It's the largest reservoir in the United States, providing water to forty million people in Nevada, Arizona, California, and beyond.

The best view of what some locals call Boulder Dam is from a pedestrian bridge along U.S. Highway 93. The hike up (a paved path with steps or a ramp) has a fun photo op: a sign showing the border between Arizona and Nevada and the Pacific and Mountain time zones.

Hoover Dam
Boulder City, no street address
Take U.S. Highway 93 southeast to Nevada Route 172
702-494-2517
usbr.gov/lc/hooverdam/service/directions.html

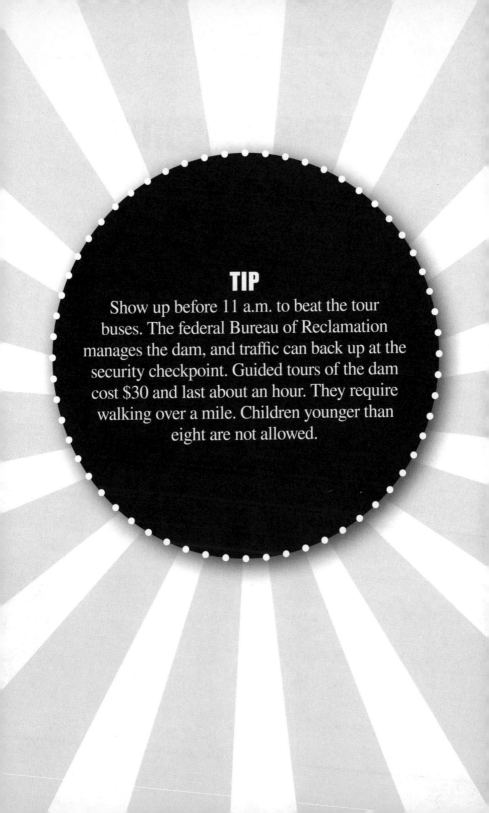

TIP

Show up before 11 a.m. to beat the tour buses. The federal Bureau of Reclamation manages the dam, and traffic can back up at the security checkpoint. Guided tours of the dam cost $30 and last about an hour. They require walking over a mile. Children younger than eight are not allowed.

WITNESS A WEDDING
OR HAVE YOUR OWN

Nevada built part of its economy on the quickie wedding—and divorce. But for the happier side of things, why don't you witness a wedding? Or if you're feeling frisky, get married yourself! Las Vegas has it all, from drive-through weddings to ceremonies where an Elvis impersonator officiates.

Swing by the wedding license bureau at the Clark County courthouse (201 E Clark Ave., Las Vegas, NV 89101) to pick up a license or see if there's a couple looking for a witness. Renewing your vows doesn't require a new license, so call the establishment first if that's your plan for a Vegas vacation.

A Little White Chapel
1301 S Las Vegas Blvd. S., Las Vegas, 702-382-5943
alittlewhitechapel.com

Chapel of the Flowers
1717 Las Vegas Blvd. S., Las Vegas, 702-735-4331
littlechapel.com

Graceland Wedding Chapel
619 S Las Vegas Blvd., Las Vegas, 702-382-0091
gracelandchapel.com

HOBNOB WITH EXPERTS
OF THE HIGHBROW AT THE
BELLAGIO ART GALLERY

Who says you can't keep it classy on the Strip? Tucked away in Bellagio is the resort's Gallery of Fine Art, and it's legit. In recent years, traveling exhibits have showcased the work of Pablo Picasso, Claude Monet, and Andy Warhol. Not too shabby. Tickets start at $19.

Gallery of Fine Art at Bellagio
3500 Las Vegas Boulevard S., Las Vegas, 702-693-7871
bellagio.com/en/entertainment/gallery-of-fine-art.html

TIP
Nevada residents can get in for almost half off—$10—on Wednesdays.

TREAT YOURSELF
TO A SPA DAY

With all the options for fun in a city like Las Vegas, making time to relax may not seem possible, but you really should. The city boasts some of the best, most luxurious spas around. Inside Canyon Ranch SpaClub at the Venetian, for example, you'll experience soothing areas such as the salt grotto, wave room, or crystal steam room. At the Mandarin Oriental spa, visitors can immerse themselves in a hammam, ice fountain, or rhassoul, among other experiences. Of course, all the spas offer a full array of massages, facials, and other indulgent services from which to choose. The hardest part will be picking which ones to order.

Canyon Ranch SpaClub
Inside The Venetian, 3355 S Las Vegas Blvd., Las Vegas, 702-414-1000
canyonranch.com

The Spa at Aria
3730 S Las Vegas Blvd., Las Vegas, 866-359-7757
aria.com

The Spa at Mandarin Oriental
3752 Las Vegas Boulevard S., Las Vegas, 888-881-9530
mandarinoriental.com

DO
THE VEGAS CELEBRITY HOUSE TOUR

Las Vegas is a city filled with headliners. Every hotel has 'em, and the city has made legends. We're talking Siegfried & Roy, Liberace, Wayne Newton, Penn & Teller here. The thing is, these legends have to sleep, right? Well, some of their houses are worth a drive by, if just to see the cool neighborhoods Vegas has to offer. Many of the houses also feature key aspects reflective of their current or former owners.

Penn Jillette's former home, The Slammer
7601 W Wigwam Ave., Las Vegas, NV 89113

Siegfried & Roy's mansion, The Jungle Palace
1639 Valley Dr., Las Vegas, NV 89108

The Liberace Mansion
4982 Shirley St., Las Vegas, NV 89119

Wayne Newton's Casa de Shenandoah (giving tours)
3310 E Sunset Rd., Las Vegas, 702-547-4811
casadeshenandoah.com

MAKE TIME
TO EXPERIENCE THE MANY CULTURAL FESTIVALS

Las Vegas is a melting pot, culturally speaking, and its many annual festivals reflect the area's population and interests. Throughout the year, Las Vegas festivals transform the landscape into ethnic food and cultural heavens. No matter your taste or style, we're sure there's one that's right up your alley. Examples of local festivals include the San Gennaro Feast, Juneteenth, Fiesta Las Vegas, Pride, Chinese New Year, Age of Chivalry Renaissance Festival, Opportunity Village's Magical Forest, the St. Patrick's Day Parade, and Ho'olaule'a Pacific Islands Festival. This isn't a comprehensive list, but you really should experience a few festivals at least once. The locals come out in droves, and it's a way to discover locally owned businesses and interact with the natives, up close and personal.

Make time to experience the many cultural festivals.

TIP
Here are a few sites that keep track of the dozens of festivals and celebrations throughout the valley:
vegas.com, everfest.com, 702events.com, vegas4locals.com

ATTEND AN OUTDOOR PERFORMANCE
AT SUPER SUMMER THEATRE

This one is hugely popular with the locals, and for good reason. Super Summer Theatre is an annual theater tradition that pairs quality shows with the great outdoors in a beautiful setting for a steal of a price. Each summer, Spring Mountain Ranch State Park hosts a handful of productions, each running a few weeks. Prices for tickets average less than $20, and everyone is welcome and encouraged to bring picnic dinners, wine, and other beverages to share and enjoy. The weather is cooler at Spring Mountain Ranch in the summer than in the Las Vegas Valley, making the evenings a beautiful and welcome respite from triple-digit heat.

Super Summer Theatre at Spring Mountain Ranch State Park
6375 Nevada 159, Blue Diamond
supersummertheatre.org

TIP
Tickets for popular performances on weekends tend to sell out, so if there's a show you really want to see, don't wait until the last minute.

JOIN A CONVERSATION
WITH CELEBRITY COLUMNIST
NORM CLARKE

Norm Clarke has written about the celebrity scene for the *Las Vegas Review-Journal* since 1999. Now, in addition to his newspaper columns, he hosts a quarterly Q-and-A with newsmakers at The Smith Center for the Performing Arts called "Conversations With Norm." Guests have included Rich Harrison of *Pawn Stars* fame, singer/comedian/impressionist Terry Fator, Las Vegas Mayor Carolyn Goodman, and her colorful husband Oscar Goodman, himself a former mayor and lawyer for the mob. Check with The Smith Center for the schedule. Proceeds benefit The Smith Center's education and outreach programming.

"Conversations With Norm"
The Smith Center for the Performing Arts
361 Symphony Park Ave., Las Vegas, 702-749-2012
thesmithcenter.com

TIP
Need more Norm? Follow him on Twitter @Norm_Clarke or check out vegasconfidential.wordpress.com

GET A LOAD OF THE BERLIN WALL,
THE BLARNEY STONE, AND THE WORLD'S LARGEST GOLD NUGGET

As if downtown Las Vegas weren't iconic enough, there are three pieces of international lore gracing its casino-hotels.

The most somber is a set of panels from the Berlin Wall, interestingly, in a men's restroom off the floor of Main Street Casino. The chunks are built into the wall behind urinals—perhaps a statement on this physical and philosophical barrier from the Cold War.

Next is a piece of the Blarney Stone, the legendary rock in Ireland that, when kissed, is said to give the gift of eloquence. This bit is on display at The D.

Last but certainly not least is the Hand of Faith, the biggest known golden nugget. The sixty-one-pound treasure was found in Australia but now is housed, appropriately, at the Golden Nugget.

Main Street Station Casino, Brewery and Hotel
200 N Main St., Las Vegas, 800-713-8933, mainstreetcasino.com

The D - Las Vegas, 301 Fremont St., Las Vegas, 702-388-2400
thed.com

Golden Nugget, 129 Fremont St., Las Vegas, 702-385-7111
goldennugget.com/lasvegas/

REFLECT ON CIVIL RIGHTS
AT THE MARTIN LUTHER KING JR. STATUE

Las Vegas pays tribute to Martin Luther King Jr. with a statue at the intersection of a street named after the civil rights icon and Carey Avenue. That corner happens to be on the northwestern border of West Las Vegas, the city's historically black neighborhood. Also included in this area are the ruins of the Moulin Rouge, on Bonanza Boulevard near the I-15 overpass. When it opened, it was billed as the first racially integrated resort in Las Vegas at a time when black performers on the Strip weren't allowed to spend the night in the casinos where they worked.

Martin Luther King Jr. statue
2428 Martin Luther King Jr. Blvd., North Las Vegas

TIP
UNLV Libraries' digital collections include the African American Experience, curating visual and oral history from Las Vegas. Learn more: digital.library.unlv.edu/aae/timeline

STEP BACK IN TIME
AT THE ATOMIC TESTING MUSEUM

Before the megaresorts, it was mushroom clouds that brought tourists. Back in the 1950s, the federal government conducted nuclear experiments in the desert about sixty-five miles north of Las Vegas, at the Nevada Test Site. Tests stopped in the 1990s, and now the bomb-pocked area is known as the Nevada National Security Site. But the nation's and the world's nuclear history is well preserved at the National Atomic Testing Museum in Las Vegas. Stop by to experience simulations and trace US policy from the Cold War to the War on Terror.

National Atomic Testing Museum
755 E Flamingo Rd., Las Vegas, 702-794-5151
nationalatomictestingmuseum.org

TIP
Still don't believe Area 51 was used just for Air Force testing? Nevada's alien lore will keep you hunting. The state went so far as rename a roadway the "Extraterrestrial Highway." Head to the town of Rachel, about 150 miles north of Las Vegas, for all the little green men souvenirs you can buy.

SHOPPING AND FASHION

BROWSE THE AISLES
WHERE THEY FILM *PAWN STARS*

You've seen it on the History Channel. Now see where your favorite pawnbrokers work. At Gold & Silver Pawn, you can buy someone else's former treasure or try your hawking skills with your favorite heirloom or knickknack. The group has a website, but wouldn't it be more fun to take a chance at making it onto the *Pawn Stars* show?

Just be prepared to wait. Show producers say they can get up to five thousand patrons a day, and there can be long lines of people and taxis.

Gold & Silver Pawn
713 Las Vegas Boulevard S., Las Vegas, 702-385-7912
gspawn.com

TIP
If the lines cut into your lunchtime, fear not.
Show star Rick Harrison opened Pawn Plaza next door,
and it has restaurants to help you pass the time.

SPEND A DAY AND NIGHT
AT BROADACRES MARKETPLACE
& EVENTS CENTER

One part swap meet and one part party, Broadacres Marketplace offers some of the best outdoor deal shopping around. At this longtime Las Vegas shopping venue, sellers pack the rows with unique items. Day or night, make sure to come hungry as the food vendors here aim to please. You'll find pupusas, Italian ices, alcohol, and lots of Mexican fare. If you go at night, there's a good chance that the onsite concert venue will be alive with banda music or another local favorite. Check out the marketplace's website for the most current information:

Broadacres Marketplace & Events Center
2930 N Las Vegas Blvd., North Las Vegas, 702-642-3777
broadacresm.com

GO RETRO
AT FANTASTIC INDOOR SWAP MEET

This place reeks retro in all the right ways. The name is technically Fantastic Indoor Swap Meet, but outside, in huge white lettering, are the words "It's Fantastik." And really, the latter spelling suits the place better. Here you'll find lots of cheap bling, art, bamboo, makeup, tools, housewares, you name it. Make it a day and enjoy the many eclectic vendors this longtime Vegas tradition has to offer. They even give you swap meet bucks at the entrance, which are discount coupons to use for purchases. The swap meet is open Friday through Sunday.

Fantastic Indoor Swap Meet
1717 S Decatur Blvd., Las Vegas, 702-877-0087
fantasticindoorswapmeet.com

GET SOME NAIL ART
BY ASHTON AT SCRATCH NAIL SPA

If you're looking to get your nails done while in Las Vegas, this is the place. Located in Henderson, Scratch Nail Spa is an unassuming nail salon from the outside. Inside, it has Ashton, the co-owner. Her co-owner, Kaitlynn, will also do a great job on your nails and toes. The duo have loads of experience and hold themselves to a high standard of artistic ability. Each has different specialties, including being able to do almost any nail art request you throw their way, all by hand. Appointments are required, but it's worth it.

Scratch Nail Spa, inside Sola Salons at The District
170 S Green Valley Parkway, #100, Ste. 12, Las Vegas
scatchnailspa.com

TIP
For sleek hairstyles, go to iBlowdry, 5120 S. Decatur Blvd., Suite 102.
Call 702-256-9379 or visit www.iblowdry.com

BUY ART
FROM A CIGARETTE MACHINE

Smoking is still allowed in Las Vegas casinos. But if you're expecting smokes in machines at the Cosmopolitan, look carefully. This resort, which works to appeal to what it calls the "curious class," uses recycled cigarette vending machines from the company Art-o-mat to sell miniature works of art. They can be small paintings or drawings or even a sculpture, as long as they're about the size of a pack of cigarettes. And they cost about as much—five bucks!

The Cosmopolitan
3708 Las Vegas Boulevard S., Las Vegas, 702-698-7000
artomat.org

VISIT
THE "WORLD'S LARGEST GIFT STORE"

Bonanza Gifts bills itself as the "World's Largest Gift Store." We can't prove the claim, but have no doubt, this place is big. At forty thousand square feet, that's about the size of a typical supermarket. And they have every kind of souvenir you could possibly need: T-shirts, mugs, keychains, pot holders, shot glasses, magnets, postcards, playing cards, and the ever classy clock decorated with dice. And most of it's pretty inexpensive. If you need some help, just ask an employee. There are lots.

Bonanza Gifts
440 Las Vegas Boulevard S., Las Vegas, 702-385-7359
worldslargestgiftshop.com

TIP
Bonanza and several other shops sell postcards for cheap.
In the email age, it can be a fun surprise to get actual mail.
For a buck—plus postage—you could really make ten people's day.

DROP SOME CASH
AT THE FINEST STORES AROUND

Las Vegas is a shoppers' paradise. From the suburban Downtown Summerlin, Tivoli Village, and Galleria at Sunset to the more central Via Bellagio, Forum Shops, Grand Canal Shoppes, and the Fashion Show Mall, Las Vegas has it all. Independent, locally owned shops mix in with large, mid- and high-end stores at Las Vegas shopping centers, giving shoppers plenty from which to choose. Jewelry, shoes, athletic equipment, pop culture buys, and pretty much anything you can dream of can be found in Las Vegas. The real trouble is just deciding where to go.

Downtown Summerlin
1980 Festival Plaza Dr., Las Vegas, 702-832-1000
downtownsummerlin.com

Tivoli Village
440 S Rampart Blvd., Las Vegas, 702-570-7400
tivolivillagelv.com

Galleria at Sunset
1300 W Sunset Rd., Henderson, 702-434-0202
galleriaatsunset.com

Town Square Las Vegas
6605 S Las Vegas Blvd., Las Vegas, 702-269-5001
mytownsquarelasvegas.com

Via Bellagio
3600 S Las Vegas Blvd., Las Vegas, 888-987-6667
bellagio.com

The Forum Shops at Caesars
3500 Las Vegas Boulevard S., Las Vegas, 702-893-4800
caesars.com

Grand Canal Shoppes
3377 S Las Vegas Blvd., Las Vegas, 702-415-4500
grandcanalshoppes.com

Fashion Show Mall
3200 S Las Vegas Blvd., Las Vegas, 702-369-8382
thefashionshow.com

THROWBACK
TO THE ANALOG AGE
AT A RECORD STORE

Some say you haven't truly heard your favorite album unless you've listened to it on vinyl. If record collecting is your thing, Las Vegas has a handful of spots for you to try.

11th Street Records
1023 Fremont St., Las Vegas, 702-527-7990
11thstreetrecords.com

Wax Trax Records Inc.
2909 S Decatur Blvd., Las Vegas, 702-362-4300
waxtraxonline.com

Record City
300 E Sahara Ave., Las Vegas, 702-735-1126
4555 E Charleston Blvd., #102, Las Vegas, 702-457-8626
recordcityonline.com

Zia Record Exchange
4503 W Sahara Avenue, 702-233-4942
4225 S Eastern Avenue, 702-735-4942
ziarecords.com

SHOP
THE SHIPPING CONTAINERS

A centerpiece of downtown Las Vegas' recent renaissance—closely linked to private investment from Zappos.com CEO Tony Hsieh—is a development that may sound odd on the surface. It's called Downtown Container Park. It's a three-story set of boutique shops, restaurants, and bars built from shipping containers. The kind you see being pulled on freight trains. You can go here for a gourmet hot dog, custom jewelry, or just to play. There's a huge treehouse with a thirty-three-foot slide, and there are periodic free concerts or movie showings.

Downtown Container Park
707 Fremont St., Las Vegas, 702-359-9982
downtowncontainerpark.com

TIP
The giant mechanical praying mantis at the entrance shoots fire. It happens unpredictably, and it might make you scream. But once you know the trick, it's fun to watch others get startled.

PERUSE VEGAS
VINTAGE SHOPS

Whether you're looking for just the right leg lamp, an old jean jacket, or a funky chair, this section of Main Street in downtown Las Vegas' arts district has plenty to sift through. Some refer to it as "Antique Alley." These three stores are in the same block.

Retro Vegas
1131 S Main St., Las Vegas, 702-384-2700
retro-vegas.com

Buffalo Exchange
1209 S Main St., Las Vegas, 702-791-3960
buffaloexchange.com

Vintage Vegas Antiques
1229 S Main St., Las Vegas, 702-539-0799

LEARN ABOUT THE NEWEST GADGETS
AT CES

Ever heard of the VCR? CD player? How about Xbox? When all these products were brand new, there was one place they were introduced to the world: CES in Las Vegas. In 2015, the show drew more than one hundred seventy thousand into 2.2 million square feet of exhibit space. That's a lot of space to showcase the world's next big inventions. You can expect drones and electric cars, but part of the fun is seeing something you never imagined.

But being close to the cutting edge comes with a price. While there are some free presentations—you have to check the schedule for that—attendance can run anywhere from a few hundred bucks to well over $1,000.

CES
cesweb.org

SEEK ART, FOOD, AND FUN
AT FIRST FRIDAY

Downtown Las Vegas streets shut down to vehicles the first Friday evening of every month to showcase local art, music, and food. As you might guess, the event is called First Friday, and thousands show up to walk among the booths and maybe meet some new friends. A good starting point is the intersection of Casino Center and Charleston Boulevards.

First Friday
fflv.net

TIP
There's plenty of parking, but you might have to pay for it.
Arrive early to find a spot on the street, or go ahead
and pay the fee for a casino or public garage.

SUGGESTED
ITINERARIES

CULTURAL CONNECTIONS

DATE NIGHT

FAMILY-FRIENDLY FUN

OUTDOOR ADVENTURES

HOLIDAY SPIRIT

INDEX

SIP LOCALLY
BREWED BEER

Look out Denver. America's craft beer renaissance is brewing in Las Vegas, too. One of the valley's best offerings is CraftHaus, based in a nondescript Henderson strip mall. The distinction is in the product: classic styles such as IPAs, browns or saisons tweaked with ingredients ranging from coffee to citrus to oak.

Of course you can find local brews linked to casinos, like Triple 7 at Main Street Station downtown, or stand-alone brew pubs like Big Dog's, serving up grub with suds.

CraftHaus Brewery
7350 Eastgate Road, Suite 110, Henderson, 702-462-5934
crafthausbrewery.com

Big Dog's Brewing Co.
4543 N. Rancho Dr., Las Vegas, 702-645-1404
bigdogsbrews.com

Triple 7 Restaurant and Microbrewery at Main Street Station
200 N. Main St., Las Vegas, 702-387-1896
mainstreetcasino.com/dine/triple-7-restaurant-and-microbrewery

TIP
If you visit CraftHaus, stop by neighbor businesses Bad Beat Brewery, Grape Expectations wine school, and Las Vegas Distillery. Together they form Henderson's Artisan Booze District. boozedistrict.com.

SAVOR SOME
SOUL FOOD

If you've got a hankering for fried catfish, collard greens, or cornbread, not surprisingly for a foodie capital, Las Vegas has some spots that will leave you feeling plenty full. Locals have favorite spots for Southern-style favorites including biscuits and gravy, chicken and waffles, chicken-fried steak, peach cobbler, and banana pudding near the Strip and off the beaten path.

Gritz Cafe
911 Stella Lake St., Las Vegas, 702-255-4748
gritzcafe.com

EllaEm's Soul Food
775 W Craig Rd., #146, North Las Vegas, 702-823-4444

M&M Soul Food Cafe
3923 W Charleston Blvd., Las Vegas, 702-453-7685

2211 Las Vegas Boulevard S., Las Vegas, 702-478-5767
mmsoulfoodcafe.com

MAKE IT
A DESSERT DATE

Whether you're looking to re-enact a rom-com scene or pair wine with post-dinner treats, Las Vegas has plenty for the perfect dessert date night. Serendipity 3 at Caesars Palace offers ice cream galore and may look familiar if you've seen the John Cusack/Kate Beckinsale movie *Serendipity*.

Off-Strip in Chinatown, check out Sweets Raku for a changing menu of pint-sized dessert courses. They can range from pie to panna cotta. The place is small, and reservations aren't accepted. Plan accordingly.

If you'd rather take your sweets to go, Sugar Factory at Planet Hollywood has extra-large sizes of all your favorite candy with brightly colored decor. For higher-end fare, see Jean Philippe Patisserie at Bellagio. Besides pastries, you can also see the Guinness-certified world's largest chocolate fountain, which sends literally tons of chocolate cascading twenty-six feet.

Serendipity 3 at Caesars Palace
3570 Las Vegas Boulevard S., Las Vegas, 702-731-7373
caesars.com/caesars-palace/restaurants/serendipity-3#.VmPhKnj09vA

Sugar Factory at Planet Hollywood Resort & Casino
3667 Las Vegas Boulevard S., Las Vegas, 702-866-0777
sugarfactory.com

Jean Philippe Patisserie at Bellagio
3600 Las Vegas Boulevard S., Las Vegas, 702-693-8788
jpchocolates.com

Sweets Raku
5040 W Spring Mountain Rd., #3, Las Vegas, 702-290-7181

GIVE RAMEN ANOTHER CHANCE

Don't let your last taste of ramen come straight out of the package. This Japanese soup—generally wheat noodles in an animal-based broth—is more than just food for broke college kids. You can get it with extra spice or other add-ons, ranging from garlic to marinated soft-boiled eggs to miso. Got questions? Just ask your server. But be prepared to wait at many of Las Vegas' favorite spots. Dining areas can be small.

Monta Ramen
5030 Spring Mountain Rd., Las Vegas, 702-367-4600

9310 S Eastern Ave., #116, Las Vegas, 702-331-5151
montaramen.com

Jinya
4860 W Flamingo Rd., Las Vegas, 702-868-8877
jinya-ramenbar.com/locations/jinya-las-vegas-2

Ramen Tatsu
3400 S Jones Blvd., Las Vegas, 702-629-7777

MORE CRAFT BREWS

LAS VEGAS

Banger Brewing Co.
450 Fremont St.
702-456-2739
bangerbrewing.com

Hop Nuts Brewing
1120 S Main St., Ste. 150
702-816-5371
hopnutsbrewing.com

Ellis Island Casino & Brewery
4178 Koval Lane
702-733-8901
ellisislandcasino.com/brewery

Old School Brewing Co.
8410 W Desert Inn Rd.
702-273-9782
oldschoolbrewing.com

Chicago Brewing Company
2201 S Fort Apache Rd.
702-254-3333

Four Queens Resort and Casino
202 Fremont St.
702-385-4011
usmenuguide.com
chicagobrewing.com

Tenaya Creek Brewery
831 W Bonanza Rd.
702-362-7335
tenayacreek.com

Sin City Brewing Co.
Grand Canal Shoppes at The Venetian
3377 Las Vegas Boulevard S.
702-629-1906

Miracle Mile Shops at Planet Hollywood
3667 Las Vegas Boulevard S.
702-732-1142

Corner of Harmon and the Strip
3717 Las Vegas Boulevard S. Ste. 210
702-749-8864
sincitybeer.com ino.com/brewery

HENDERSON

Barley's Casino and Brewing Co.
4500 E Sunset Rd.
702-458-2739
wildfire.sclv.com/Barleys

Bad Beat Brewery
7380 Eastgate Rd., Ste. 110
702-463-4199
badbeatbrewing.com

Joseph James Brewing Co.
155 N Gibson Rd.
702-454-2739
jjbrewing.com

ENJOY A MEAL AL FRESCO

Much of the Strip might have been designed to keep you in a casino, but Las Vegas has plenty of places to enjoy a meal outdoors. Many restaurants that offer al fresco dining use misters to cool the air during the summer. In winter, they put out heaters. Here are a few spots with tasty food worth eating in the open air.

Echo and Rig at Tivoli Village
440 S Rampart Blvd., Las Vegas, 702-489-3525
echoandrig.com

Mon Ami Gabi at Paris Las Vegas
3655 Las Vegas Boulevard S., Las Vegas, 702-944-4224
monamigabi.com

Park on Fremont
506 Fremont St., Las Vegas, 702-834-3160
parkonfremont.com

TIP
At Park on Fremont, walk behind the back wall to find a seesaw.
Take a friend and hop on!